Ghosts *of* Kennecott

The Story of Stephen Birch

Elizabeth A. Tower

ublication Consultants

PO Box 221974 Anchorage, Alaska 99522-1974

ISBN 1-59433-007-7

Library of Congress Catalog Card Number: 2003113762

Copyright 2003 by Elizabeth A. Tower
—Second Edition—

*Front Cover Design by Suzanne Mitchell and
Hal Gage, Gage Photo Graphics, Anchorage, Alaska*

ACKNOWLEDGMENTS

The author extends special thanks for the assistance of the following people: The staff of the Kennecott Library in Salt Lake City for assistance in the on-site examination of records and correspondence files; William Collins, great-nephew of Stephen Birch, for information on the Birch family (Stephen Birch has no surviving direct descendants); Maria Skala, postgraduate student at Alaska Pacific University, for sharing materials collected for her master's thesis.

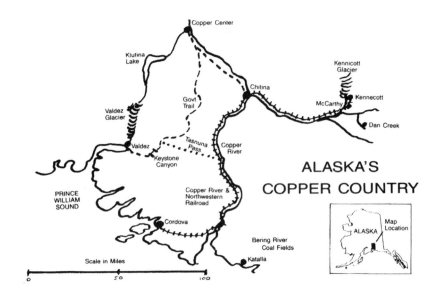

ALASKA'S
COPPER COUNTRY

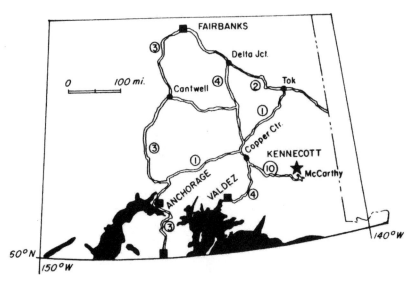

Current highway routes to Kennecott.

Contents

Stephen Birch, 1872-1940 *Courtesy of Kennecott Library*

Birch's start in life did not promise future wealth. Born in 1872, he was the second son of a wounded Union Army sergeant, who died when Stephen was ten years old and his youngest brother, George Howard, not yet born. Three years after her husband's death, Birch's widowed mother moved with her six children from Brooklyn to Mahwah, New Jersey, to be near relatives. The young Birches soon became friends and sporting companions of the children of their neighbors, Theodore Havemeyer, the vice-president of American Sugar Refining Company, and his wife, Lillie. Mrs. Havemeyer took a special interest in young Stephen, providing financial assistance for his education at Trinity School, New York University, and Columbia School of Mines.

ABERCROMBIE EXPEDITION — 1898

At the peak of the Klondike gold rush in 1898, Stephen announced that he wanted to go to Alaska rather than continue working with an engineering team that was surveying for the New York City subway system. Most of his friends and relatives failed to take him seriously, but Mrs. Havemeyer offered to finance his trip to Valdez, a newly-established city hailed as the port for an all-American route to Alaska's interior. The Pacific Packing and Navigation Company promoted this gateway to the gold fields and succeeded in persuading several thousand argonauts to book passage to Valdez and ascend Valdez glacier, thus avoiding Skagway where Soapy Smith and his gang controlled access to the passes.

When H.O. Havemeyer II realized that his mother and Birch were serious, he and several associates agreed to pay expenses and arrange for a proper connection so there would be no worry about Birch's care and safety.[1] As a result of the intervention of his wealthy friends, Birch arrived in Valdez early in the summer of 1898 with a request to Capt. W.R. Abercrombie that he be attached to Abercrombie's Copper River Exploring Expedition in a civilian capacity. Abercrombie, whom President William McKinley had detailed to explore potential All-American routes to the Interior, was not impressed that the Easterner was a suitable participant in his wilderness scouting expedition. Birch, displaying the singleness of purpose that distinguished his later career, took the first steamer back to Seattle and contacted his influential sponsors, who protested to Washington D.C. Abercrombie was incensed when Birch returned to Valdez, and told him:

"Maybe I can't fire you but I can throw you out of my office."[2]

By this time Abercrombie could scarcely afford to be choosy. He had initially planned to use reindeer as pack animals for his military reconnaissance expedition. The deer had been purchased in Lapland the winter before, shipped across the Atlantic, carried by railroad to Seattle, and then by ship to Haines. Reindeer moss ran out in the course of the lengthy journey and

"The All-American Routes to the Valley of the Yukon." from the *Seattle Post -Intelligencer*. March 18, 1998

many deer died. When Abercrombie reached Haines, he found the surviving deer too debilitated to be of use and went on to Valdez without pack animals. Realizing that men could not carry all the needed equipment, Abercrombie had to send to Seattle for pack horses, thus delaying the start of a party to establish a route from Valdez to the Yukon River.

As a result of this delay, Birch was back in Valdez in early July when the expedition was finally ready to start. Illness had depleted the army detachment. Only two officers were still healthy, Abercrombie and Lieutenant P.G. Lowe. In his official report, Abercrombie described Lowe's part in the expedition:

> Lt. Lowe is a man to be killed but not conquered... He was directed to organize a party, consisting of himself and three men, with ten head of stock, and to proceed at once to Forty-Mile River via Mentasta Pass, with a view to locating an all-American route from Valdez to the Yukon. On consulting with Lt. Lowe it was decided that the course of duty lay over the glacier even if all the stock and some of the men were lost in making the attempt.

Valdez Glacier— All-American Routes to Alaska's Interior 1998
Courtesy of Anchorage Museum of History and Art B62-1-1293

Birch was one of the civilian guides assigned to accompany Lowe on his reconnaissance expedition. After an initial unsuccessful attempt to scale the glacier, the men left Valdez on July 13, 1898, accompanied by some army troops to help get the horses through the rotten crevasse-filled ice field. Lowe told of the hazardous trip over Valdez Glacier in his official report:

> By zigzagging I was enabled to find points along the crevasses narrow enough for the horses to jump over. In many places the snow covered the ice, and

the crevasses were not discovered until some of the horses had gotten a leg or two in them. Every horse managed to get one or two legs in a number of times, and they practically hung by their "eyebrows." At times it required the prompt and united efforts of the entire party to rescue them. One horse was saved by his pack striking the edge of the crevasse behind him, when he had both legs in. Had the animal not been sensible and quiet he would have struggled into some other position and gone down for good.

Third Bench Camp on Valdez Glacier. 1898 *Courtesy of Anchorage Museum of History and Art B62-1-1343*

This same horse probably saved the life of Private Hilliard, of the Fourteenth Infantry. The latter went down, but held to the horse's shanks, while the animal braced himself and the man climbed out. ...After some pretty stiff floundering the expedition managed to get through, but we had not an inch too much snow under us.

When the expedition reached the Klutina River, the additional men returned to Valdez, leaving Lowe and the civilian employees to continue with the horses. Although they were using a prospector's trail, several of the men frequently went ahead to clear brush and find safe places to ford streams. Traveling in this manner, they reached the Copper River at Copper Center on July 31, and Lowe reported:

> Copper Center is a sort of interior starting point, the objective appearing to be the headwaters of the Copper and the Tanana. ... Quite a number of cabins were in course of construction; but more than half of the people who had come over the glacier had returned home disheartened, and I met no less than 200 returning prospectors between the glacier and Copper Center. The fabulous wealth of the country had been well advertised, but, the prospectors not finding any gold, the disappointment was too much for them. There may be gold in the Copper River country, but up to the time I passed through it none had been discovered, although several alarms had been sounded. The country was advertised before it was tested.

The men had traveled 100 miles over a known trail to reach Copper Center and had 300 more miles to go through unknown country. Maps that were available proved to be worthless, and the people they talked to told conflicting stories about the terrain ahead.

The first obstacle to cross was the Copper River, as described by Lowe:

> Finally I came to the conclusion that, although the animals could in ordinary water be induced to attempt swimming the distance, the swiftness of the current, as well as the extreme coldness of the water, would cause them to turn back. Believing that swimming them behind a skiff would be in every way better, I made a successful test with some of the best water animals. I swam them to an island, and from there they were led behind a boat, two at a time, with a man in the stern attending to each horse.

After crossing the Copper River for the first time, they followed an indistinct prospector trail across the big bend of the Copper until they came to the mouth of the Slana River. Here they had to cross the Copper again, but, since there was no settlement, boats were not readily available to help. Lowe's report contained this mention of Birch's participation in the crossing attempt:

> On August 14, I succeeded in finding a ford through an island half a mile below camp... On the following day I moved with my outfit to the island and proceeded to make a raft with which to cross the main channel of the river. My tools were three axes and an auger. The raft was finished and launched the following day and the occupants, lightly clad, started for the opposite bank on the trial trip. The channel was about 30 yards wide, the current very swift, and the raft was immediately at its mercy. To pole was the original intention, but it became evident that oars only could be used, and that a landing must be effected on any shore possible. The raft passed close to the home shore and Birch jumped with the rope; but his feet were instantly swept from under him and he found himself in deep water. He was very cool, however, and held to the rope until hauled on board.

While the group was reassessing their plans, a boat luckily came downstream and they were able to get help again in crossing a major river.

After this crossing, the expedition left the Copper River and followed the Slana up to an Indian settlement on Mentasta Lake, where two English- speaking Natives gave them information about the trail ahead. After crossing Meiklejohn Pass into the Tanana River drainage, they reached an Indian settlement where the Tetling River flows into the Tanana, and employed the chief's son to act as a guide. Two of the villagers who owned canoes postponed a caribou hunting trip to help the expedition cross the Tanana River . Lowe registered his doubts about the journey ahead:

... We had now burned our bridges behind us, as the Indians were off for their annual caribou hunt, and the distance in any event back to Valdez was so much greater than that to the Yukon that the latter became the preferable objective. Upon leaving the Tanana we entered a country that had not been mapped from actual observation. Information was obtained from the Indians and the country was mapped as well as the imagination could allow. An Indian will tell you it is so many "sleeps" to a certain place, packing so many pounds on your pack, but he can not tell you the number of miles, and as there is a difference in the endurance of Indians there is a difference in the number of "sleeps."

The men soon found that the information obtained from the Indians was more accurate than the army maps they were attempting to follow. Their objective was a store at the junction of Miller Creek and the Sixty-Mile River where they hoped to get information about where they could find a good beaten trail to the Yukon River. For the next two weeks they continued to travel between branches of the Sixty-Mile and Forty-Mile Rivers with the horses getting weaker and the nights colder. When unpacking after a day in the cold rain, Lowe noted that "the hands of my party were so numb that it was hard to handle the ropes and it took three times the ordinary time required to get camp in shape." One of the horses had to be abandoned before they reached Miller Creek, and four more when they encountered a snow storm between Miller Creek and Forty-Mile River.

Once the expedition reached the Forty-Mile River, they were able to buy a boat in which to cover the remaining 26 miles to the settlement of Forty- Mile. The river passed through a tortuous canyon, so they left the horses behind with one of the civilian employees who was planning to spend the winter in the area. After lining the boat down one rapid and shooting another, they arrived at the cabin village on the Yukon on September 25.

Since it was too late to catch the last boat for St. Michaels, the group was fortunate to find two American boats that were pushing a barge with supplies for Canadian troops at Fort Selkirk. The expedition landed at Dawson on September 26, and several days later took the *W.K. Merwinx* up river, arriving at the White Horse Rapids on October 15. Lowe described the final days of the expedition:

> The steamer *Nora* was boarded in the afternoon and started for the head of Lake Bennett, but came near having to shoot Miles Canyon and the rapids before getting under way. As the bow left the shore the wheel got tangled in a raft and could not revolve without tearing off the buckets. For the ship to float down as she was and land would be to tear her bottom off on the rocks. Her nose swung down with the current and was run into the opposite bank the moment she was free. She was tied up, given a chance to breathe, and started on her way again. Lake Marsh and Six-Mile River were passed and the boat tied up at an important police post on Tagish Lake.
>
> October 16 the head of Lake Bennett was reached, which is a thriving village with many hotels and an important police station. The day following the expedition sent its baggage to White Pass by pack train and walked 8 miles over the Skagway trail to Log Cabin, a large village of cabins and tents. The trail was fair, although wet.
>
> October 18 the expedition walked 20 miles to White Pass, which is quite a town, but will soon disappear, as the railroad is passing around it... The Trail is rocky, muddy, rough, and about as bad as possible... The members of the expedition would occasionally step on dead horses and hogs... After 20 miles of stiff walking the expedition entered a canyon that surpassed for beauty and grandeur anything that had been seen. In the afternoon the members of the expedition boarded the narrow-gauge railroad and rode 12 miles into Skagway .

Stephen Birch returned to New York. He had survived his first summer in Alaska and was hardened to the trail.

BONANZA DISCOVERY — 1900

W hen the Copper River Exploring Expedition returned to Alaska in the spring of 1899, Capt. Abercrombie had no chance to reject Birch. His orders from G.D. Meiklejohn, Assistant Secretary of War, stated:

> Capt. W.R. Abercrombie, Second Infantry, commanding Copper River Exploring Expedition, accompanied by Stephen Birch, guide, will proceed at once to Fort Keogh and Livingston, Mont., there inspect, accept, and brand such pack horses, not to exceed 30 head, as come up to the required standard. On completion of this duty Captain Abercrombie, accompanied by Guide Birch, will proceed to Seattle, Wash. The travel enjoined is necessary for the public service.[3]

Although he is not mentioned again in Abercrombie's official report of the 1899 expedition, Birch presumably spent the summer of 1899 around Valdez and the Copper River country as a horse-packer for the army during the building of a military road through Keystone Canyon and over Thompson Pass.

When Abercrombie arrived at Valdez he found a desperate situation. Many of the 4,000 prospectors who had attempted to enter Alaska over Valdez Glacier had already perished or returned home disillusioned. Some who remained in Valdez over the winter were ravaged by scurvy, and they reported that others in the interior were also suffering from the lack of fresh food. In addition to his other duties, Abercrombie provided antiscorbutics and medical attention to the ailing prospectors.

Some prospectors who were still physically able accompanied the army expedition into the Chitina River valley in hopes of locating the source of copper bullets that the Taral Chief Nicolai had shown Lieutenant Allen on a previous army ex-

Unloading horses at Valdez. *Courtesy of Alaska State Library, PCA192-7*

pedition. Included in the group were ten men led by Rueben McClellan, a rugged frontiersman from Minnesota. This McClellan group, which in the coming years would play a crucial role in Birch's career, had agreed to pool their interests in prospecting so that any discovery made by a member would be shared by all. Membership in the group varied from time to time and the arrangement was further complicated because some of the members were also grubstaked with food and equipment from other sources.

When the McClellan group and another group led by B.F. Millard succeeded in reaching the village of Taral, they found Chief Nicolai and his people close to starvation. Nicolai agreed to reveal the location of his mine in return for the prospectors' cache of food.[4] This outcropping of ore, located on a small tributary of McCarthy Creek, proved to contain up to 85 per cent copper. These Nicolai claims, staked in July 1899, were the first copper claims in the area.

After the prospecting season of 1899 ended, the McClellan group met in Valdez and decided that some of them, including McClellan, would return home for the winter, while others, including Clarence Warner and "Tarantula" Jack Smith would remain in Alaska to prospect during the winter and return to the vicinity of the Nicolai claims the following spring. At this time they decided to make Major Abercrombie a share holder in the McClellan group, presumably for the assistance he had provided that summer. They also started to negotiate consolidation of the Nicolai claims for development, with McClellan representing his group and B.F. Millard, H.G. Allis, and George M. Perine the other interests.[5]

After visiting his home in Princeton, Minnesota, McClellan met Millard and Perine in San Francisco and transferred the interests of his group in the Nicolai Mine to the newly formed Chittyna Exploration Company in return for 150 shares of stock in that company, which was then divided among the original members of the McClellan company and some of the people who had grubstaked them. While in San Francisco, Millard and Perine asked McClellan to be superintendent of the company's affairs in Alaska during the summer of 1900.

McClellan landed in Valdez on April 17, 1900, accompanied by a dozen hired men and an equal number of horses, all purchased with Chittyna Exploration Company funds to do the assessment and development work on the Nicolai claims. In the meanwhile, Smith and Warner, along with two other members of the McClellan party who had spent the winter in Alaska, left Valdez on March 2 for the Chitina country pulling hand sleds over Valdez Glacier. These men, who had no knowledge of the formation of the Chittyna Exploration Company, continued prospecting in the Chitina River valley during the summer of 1900 as members of the McClellan group.[6]

In July, Smith and Warner were prospecting in the vicinity of Mt. Blackburn at the headwaters of the Kennicott River when they located the outcropping of copper ore that led to the for-

Prospectors pushing sleds over glacier. *Courtesy of Alaska State Library, PCA159-15*

mation of the Kennecott Copper Company. In a letter to Alaska Territorial Governor Ernest Gruening, written in January 1940, Stephen Birch gave this description of the Bonanza discovery:

> They (Smith and Warner) made four locations the second day after they had established their camp. These locations were known as the Independence 1 and 2, Excelsior and National. After they had made them, and while sitting eating their lunch, they looked across the

gulch and observed a large green spot on the side of the mountain. Jack's companion declared it was a patch of grass. Jack was not certain and said he would like to go over and see it, but his companion wasn't going to climb up the side of that mountain to look at a sheep pasture. While discussing this they became thirsty and Jack went down to the creek to get some water. While leaning over the bank he saw a piece of float — float is the name given by prospectors to a small piece of rock containing mineral. Jack at first did not know whether it was copper or silver. He took back the piece to his companion, and they agreed to follow up the creek looking for more green rock as they went. Gradually as they came near the green patch in the mountain the float became thicker, and presently they saw that instead of being a grass plot it was an outcropping of copper ore. When he saw the size of it, Jack exclaimed, "My God, it's a bonanza!" So then and there it was named the "Bonanza."

This was on July 22, 1900. After they had made their location, they returned to their camp and as their provisions were about all gone it was necessary for them to return to Valdez, a distance of 200 miles. This they were obliged to walk, as they had no horses or other means of transportation.

During the fall the other members of the McClellan party returned to Valdez with reports from various parts of the country, but none of them had been so successful as Jack. The entire party's interest was centered on the great copper discovery, and it was agreed among them to try to interest capital.[7]

Stephen Birch, who was in Valdez when the McClellan group returned from their summer of prospecting, was one of the people they approached about financing. Birch had returned to New York the previous winter and continued his studies as a special student at Columbia University. His friends Henry Havemeyer and James Ralph then sent him back to Valdez to look for investment opportunities. Birch's own account of his meeting with the prospectors is contained in the letter to Gruening:

Jack brought his find to my attention. "Mr. Birch", he said, "I've got a mountain of copper up there. There's so much of the stuff sticking out of the ground that it looks like a green sheep-pasture in Ireland when the sun is shining at its best." But it was too late in the year to go in and examine it, so it was agreed that I should go in the next season, make a proper survey and report to my principals. The latter, on the other hand, agreed if the mine was as represented to put up money for its development.

Birch had confidence in the prospectors of the McClellan group and was willing to start negotiations with them even before he could investigate the claims. The opportunity came in early November 1900 when he received a letter from Dan Kain, one of the McClellan group, offering to sell one half of his one-eleventh interest to Birch. On December 2 Birch wrote to Havemeyer:

> The man who wrote the enclosed letter offered to sell me half of his interest in a number of claims for $2,000 which is dirt cheap. ... I am anxious to get things settled so that I can telegraph him, otherwise he will be apt to sell to some one else.
> Now is the time to make a barrel of money. ... After we get hold of these claims we can either sell things to the Lewisohns or some other company or make a deal to go in with them and form a big company.[8]

On December 9 Birch informed Havemeyer that he had closed the deal with Dan Kain, paying him $250 immediately. The final contract provided for Birch to pay $2,500 for a half interest in Kain's property, including his one-eleventh share in the McClellan group claims and all other claims made by Kain for the next three years. In a January letter to Kain, Birch explained:

> This I think is a fair work deal to both you and myself. It will give you ready money and me a good speculation and is a better proposition for both of us as you get more money and I get larger interest. I

will be on the ground and we can mutually assist each other.[9]

The contractual arrangement proved particularly advantageous to Birch because Kain subsequently located rich placer gold claims on a tributary of the Nizina River, named Dan Creek in his honor. Kain promised to use his influence with other members of the McClellan group to help Birch obtain options on their claims as well, but insisted that Birch make no mention of the terms of his contract. In early February Kain wrote Birch:

> I want you to promise me not to use any information you have received through me unless you have my permission. Do this for me and it will make my work easy with our party and I assure you I will do my best to serve you.[10]

Birch was equally anxious to assure Havemeyer that, although the negotiations with Kain had been done in Birch's name, he was only acting as an agent for Havemeyer. On December 31, 1900, he wrote Havemeyer:

> I deeply appreciate the interest you take in this matter and feel that you are actuated because of your desire to aid me, and I will not make any arrangements unless they are satisfactory to you.

Havemeyer and Ralph formed the Alaska Copper Company, incorporated in West Virginia, and Birch was placed on a retainer of $300 monthly plus expenses.

Birch returned to Valdez early in the spring of 1901 to make a personal inspection of the Bonanza claims. He gave the following retrospective account of this trip in the 1940 letter to Gruening:

> In April 1901, I started in with R.F. McClellan. There were no trails in the country and we had to travel on foot a distance of more than 200 miles. It was a hard trip as I think of it now, but mining engineers are prepared for that kind of thing.

The rest of the McClellan party had gone in during the winter months, sledding in the necessary supplies to live on while they did the annual assessment work as required by the Government.

For the first hundred miles we dragged a hand sled packed with blankets and provisions, but when we got to the Copper River the snow had left the valleys and we abandoned the sled and employed Indians to pack the supplies on their backs. That was really an interesting 100 miles.

I remained at the mine during the season, making various examinations and tests of the ore. Then I returned to New York and reported favorably to my principals. They then optioned the property from the McClellan party and agreed to spend money on its development.

This account makes the acquisition of the claims from the other members of the McClellan party sound easier than it actually was. Birch spent most of the next winter traveling around the country contacting members of the McClellan group to obtain options. On March 6, *The Alaska Prospector* in Valdez reported:

There has been some fear in the minds of many persons that the reported sale of the famous McClellan copper properties in the Chittyna River country was merely "talk", started in order to con the country, but such is not the case, as there was filed for record in the U.S. commissioner's office a few days ago a number of optional agreements, deeds and other papers agreeing to sell about ten-elevenths of the entire McClellan property as it is generally known in this place, for the sum of $1,100,000.

These agreements are from R.F. McClellan, E.A. Gates, H.H. Fitch, W.S. Amy, Dan L. Kain, Jno.L. Sweeney, J.H. Smith, C.L. Warner, H.T. Gates and Stephen Birch, and the property agreed to be conveyed consists of 45 copper claims in the Chittyna country.

This account with the financial details of the options was

probably given to the Valdez paper by Birch himself. A letter to Havemeyer on March 3 tells of his landing at Valdez and making the arrangements for patenting the claims. Birch's arrival in Valdez had been delayed for two weeks because he was a passenger on the steamer *Bertha* when it ran aground in Fitzhugh Channel on February 9. The *Daily Alaska Dispatch* gives the following account of the mishap:

> All went well with the *Bertha* until Saturday night, when the weather set in thick, and Sunday morning at 12:30 the vessel struck on Harald Island. All the

SS *Bertha* on the rocks — February 1902 *Courtesy of Anchorage Museum of History and Art B62-1-381*

passengers were in bed, and the shock caused great confusion and a stampede was made for the upper deck. Captain Johnson and the officers of the ship restored order in short time, and on investigation it was found that the vessel was in such close proximity to the shore that the gangplank would reach an elevated rock. The passengers at once walked ashore, and later bedding and baggage were landed, and a camp was made on barren rocks.

On the approach of daylight the work of lightering the vessel was commenced by landing horses and other freight. A kedge anchor was put out, and the vessel hauled into deep water with aid of the donkey engine, but as soon as deep water was struck she began to sink. The vessel was swung on the beach. She has lost her keel, and there is a large hole in her bottom forward engine room and it is believed she will be a total loss.

The first night the passengers camped on the rock they suffered no serious inconvenience, but on the second day a heavy rain set in, with a cold wind, which caused considerable suffering, as the wind swept across the rock with great force. Monday morning the shipwrecked folk were picked up by the *Cottage City* and brought to this place (Port Townsend). The loss of freight and baggage, by exposure to the elements, after being landed, is a severe blow to many, as they had their last dollar invested in outfits for the season's prospecting in Alaska.

Dan Kain was one of the prospectors who lost his outfit in the grounding of the *Bertha*, but Birch advanced him money for more supplies and was reimbursed by the Alaska Copper Company.

Birch wrote Havemeyer on March 8 thanking him for reassuring his mother of his safety after the shipwreck, and again on the following day registering concern for the lack of a safe place for keeping records of claims and deeds. "The way it is now," he wrote, "they are kept on shelves in a wooden building over a saloon. There is always a lot of intoxicated men hanging around both day and night. It is the worst building in town in case of fire. It would play the devil with us if the records should burn up." He went on to urge Havemeyer to have someone contact Attorney General Knox and try to get a safe for the Valdez court.[11]

After registering this concern, Birch left for the mine, writing Havemeyer from Tonsina Bridge on March 24 to tell of his progress. A letter written at the mine site on April 19 tells Havemeyer of his arrival and plans to build a cabin and some mountain trails. Birch had lots of work to do during the summer of 1902 in order to prepare for the visit of a group of mining experts, who were coming to assess the potential for both copper and gold mining in the Chitina and Nizina area.

On July 10 *The Alaska Prospector* announced the arrival of this party of mining experts, which included H.A. Keller of Seattle, M.J. Heller of San Francisco, F.H. Blake of New York, and Norris English of San Francisco. The group first toured copper mining sites on Prince William Sound and then met Birch in Valdez for an expedition to the Nicolai and Bonanza claims. On September 4, *The Alaska Prospector* reported the group's return to Valdez, and commented: "Mr. Stephen Birch had charge of the expedition and managed it so well that the trip seemed like a picnic."

The experts were, apparently, pleased with what they saw. Upon return from the mine in the fall, Birch began actually purchasing the claims from the prospectors in the McClellan

Mining experts at future site of Kennecott Mines. Stephen Birch second from left — July 1902 *Courtesy National Archives*

group. A series of letters to Havemeyer in November indicate that Birch had to travel to Minnesota, California and Arizona in order to exercise the options. The Alaska Copper Company kept him supplied with ready cash so he was able to purchase most of the interests for between $12,000 and $15,000. The largest cash outlay was $25,000 which Birch paid for W.S. Amy's share. While everything was going according to Birch's plan for gaining ownership of the Bonanza claims, another problem had arisen. The September

11, 1902 issue of *The Alaska Prospector* contained the following announcement:

> Notice has been filed in the commissioner's office that suit will be brought by the Chittyna ExplorationCo. against R.F. McClellan and others who are interested in the Alaska Copper Co. for an interest in the Bonanza group of claims. The suit has been brought by the Exploration Company on the

Loading horses for Winchell party. *Courtesy of Alaska State Library, PCA159-5*

> grounds that the locators of the said claims were in the employ of the company at the time locations were made.
>
> All the parties concerned, who are now here, are very reticent about the matter, and refuse to be interviewed on the subject.

BONANZA LAWSUIT — 1903

The filing of a lawsuit over ownership of the Bonanza claims focused nationwide attention on the potential for copper mining in the Wrangell Mountains. Both sides in the controversy enlisted the support of influential people and additional capital. Birch and Havemeyer, facing a large cash outlay for buying the claims and hiring lawyers, enlisted leather-king Norman Schultz as a major investor and changed the name of their corporation to Alaska

George Hazelet — Anaconda Expedition Guide. *Courtesy of Alaska State Library, PCA159-2*

Copper and Coal to avoid confusion with another copper corporation with holdings in Southeast Alaska. The Chittyna Mining Company, in the meantime, sold its claim to the Bonanza locations to a wealthy syndicate, the Copper River Mining Company, organized specifically to pursue the lawsuit.

Other copper-producing companies also showed interest

in the potential for mining in Alaska. In the summer of 1903, Horace V. Winchell, the chief geologist for Anaconda Copper Company, brought a group of experts to Alaska to assess development potentials. The group, which included Lewis A. Levensaler, visited the Beatson Copper Mines on LaTouche Island and enlisted George Hazelet and his pack-train to lead them into the Chitina River country. Birch, who returned to Alaska the previous February to continue work at the mine, mentioned in a June 22, 1903 letter to Havemeyer that Schultz and his lawyer had instructed him not to let anyone near the mine. Birch responded, "I shall keep them off unless they take me by storm", and he succeeded in keeping the Anaconda party from seeing the Bonanza Mine. Levensaler later joined Birch in developing the Kennecott Mines.

The lawyers involved in the Bonanza lawsuit were also busy that summer taking depositions in New York, San Francisco, Manila, and other distant places. Birch commented in a November 9, 1903 letter to Havemeyer that Senator Heyburn of Idaho, Congressman Cushing of Washington, and Andrew Burleigh, some of the attorneys for the opposition, arrived in Valdez on October 29 accompanied by "a number of professional witnesses and thugs." "The first thing after their arrival," he continued, "they started right in to blow themselves at the various saloons and tried to create a favorable impression on the community."[12] Judge James Wickersham, who was hearing the case, also participated in the socialization. He wrote in his diary on October 23 that his wife had invited Birch, McClellan, and some of the lawyers on both sides of the case to a whist party.

Wickersham heard the Bonanza Case in November, mentioning in his diary that he was reading more than 2000 pages of testimony taken by deposition.

On November 28, Wickersham wrote in the diary:

> Rendered decision in Copper Co. v McClellan et. al., the celebrated Chitina River copper case. Senator Heyburn of Idaho, Congressman Cushman of Wash., Burleigh of N.Y. etc. were attorneys for plaintiff — decided case for the defendant on grounds that plaintiffs testimony was not sufficient. Great crowd in attendance.

The plaintiffs in the case had argued that the locators of the claims were either grubstaked by or employees of the Chittyna Exploration Company when they staked the Bonanza claims. McClellan summarized the case in a Seattle interview for the November 29, 1903 *The Post-Intelligencer*:

> The controversy over the Bonanza Mine was originally instigated by the Chittyna Exploration Company, but that organization subsequently sold its claim to a title in the property to the Copper River Mining Company, which was organized for the purpose of making a fight for control of the mine.

James Wickersham, Judge of Third Judicial District during Bonanza Trial. *Courtesy of Alaska State Library, PCA277-7-167*

To understand the situation one must know that

the so-called McClellan crowd, which located the Bonanza, was organized and went to Alaska in 1898. We prospected in various parts of the country, and finally made some valuable discoveries in the Chittyna valley. The Chittyna Exploration Company was organized to develop some of these properties, and we retained a one-fourth interest in the new company. In 1900 I was made superintendent of the Nicolai Mine, which the Chittyna Exploration Company decided to develop.

There were at this time ten members of the "McClellan crowd." When I took the superintendency of the Nicolai Mine, two members of the party returned to the states and the other seven went off on prospecting tours. These seven prospectors were working in the interests of the ten members of my party. We furnished our own money to back ourselves and did our own work. J.H. Smith and C.L. Warner located the Bonanza Mine in July 1900.

No one ever disputed our title to the Bonanza until 1901, when we endeavored to bond the property. Even then offers were made to me by other claimants to purchase the property outright, as if we owned it beyond any shadow of an adverse claim. But we were anxious to develop the property, and were working at the time to interest the Havemeyers, as we afterwards succeeded in doing. They bonded the property for $1,100,000, or $100,000 less than the parties who afterward organized the Copper River Mining Company and disputed our claim offered to give me.

The Chittyna Exploration Company set up a claim for the property. The first contention of the corporation was that they had grubstaked our party and the exploration company was entitled to a half interest. This position was abandoned, and they claimed that our party were in the Chittyna ExplorationCompany's employ and that organization was entitled to undisputed ownership of the Bonanza. ...

We showed conclusively that I was the only member of our party that was employed by the Chittyna Exploration Company. The men who located Bonanza had never worked for that company. In fact five of party had never worked for wages while in Alaska. We showed that instead of the Chittyna company grubstaking our party, we had actually given that company provisions to keep the crew at work. This disposed of any shadow of a claim that the Copper River Mining Company had in the Bonanza.

I am told that large blocks of the Copper River Mining Company were sold in Pennsylvania and New York, and that just a short time ago $37,000 was borrowed by the company. In fact, a mortgage given on the Bonanza was sent to Valdez for record. Of course, the court's decree shows that this company has no right to give such a mortgage nor to sell stock.

The parties who we believe put up this fight and who provided the evidence that induced reputable attorneys to make their contest are promoters, headed by F.C. Helm, who is known here. Helm had a railroad and numerous other enterprises projected which he declared would be built in Alaska by his company.

I know the victory of our company means more to the Copper River country than anything that has happened there for years. The Bonanza Mine has demonstrated that it will be a valuable freight producer, and the Havemeyers, abundantly able to provide means for the construction of a railroad, will see that one is built. A railroad into the Copper River country is now practically assured.

We have done comparatively little development work, though we have been in undisputed possession of the property. Our company did not care to put out the money necessary for the improvement while the title was in controversy, but we have a tunnel that has struck the vein ninety feet below the surface where the men, at the last time I heard from the mine, had cut through seven feet of copper and had not passed the vein. There are thousands of tons of ore lying on the surface, and it has been estimated that the property shows $17,000,000 of copper in sight. This of course is an estimated valuation, but we know that there are millions of dollars' worth of ore to be taken out and I believe the Bonanza will prove to be the richest mine in Alaska.

Now that the title is settled we will push development work as rapidly as possible. Arrangements will be made for the construction of a railroad into the interior and the entire Copper River valley will be benefited.

McClellan was premature in his prediction of prompt development of the mine and railroad construction. Wickersham's decision in the Bonanza Case was appealed to higher courts. The financiers were reluctant to proceed with extensive investments until ownership was assured. Furthermore reports from the Anaconda experts raised doubts about the value of the Bonanza ore deposits in spite of the prior, more optimistic, assessment.

Birch and Wickersham became good friends during the course of the Bonanza Case and left Valdez together on December 4 along with other participants in the trial. Wickersham makes special mention in his diary that Birch left the *Santa Ana* at Ladysmith B.C. on December 16. Four days later they were together again in Washington D.C. where Wickersham and his wife were attending the graduation of their son, Darrell, from the U.S. Naval Academy.

Wickersham's term as a district judge was about to expire and he stayed in the Washington area in an effort to enlist congressional support for his reappointment. Birch was one of the friends who helped Wickersham to make valuable contacts, and on January 17, 1904, Wickersham commented in the diary: "Stephen Birch from New York is here today at the Raleigh — working for me." His January 20 diary stated: "Birch is back to the Raleigh — I moved down there today that I might have more time before I go away." Birch also invited Wickersham to New York, where they dined at Delmonicos, attended several Broadway plays, and met with Birch's financial backers, James Ralph and Norman Schultz .

Finally, on November 17, 1904, Wickersham received word that the President had reappointed him judge of the third division in Alaska. The same day he received a telegram from Birch stating: "We all send hearty congratulations on your reappointment." Along with other letters of congratulation, a letter from Senator Knute Nelson of Minnesota, the powerful chairman of the Committee on Territories, prompted Wickersham to comment in his diary: "He is still ugly — but not virulent — He keeps harping upon the idea that Birch supports me — as if a successful litigant ought to be expected to abuse the court."

Senator Nelson continued to be ugly where Wickersham was concerned, leading the opposition to Senate confirmation of the reappointment. Wickersham's failure to support Nelson's effort to split Alaska's third judicial district had angered the senator.[13]

For the next two years Nelson and several other senators used all means in their power, including filibuster, to block Wickersham's confirmation. President Roosevelt, however, continued to keep

Capt. David Jarvis, Treasurer of Alaska Syndicate. *Copied from a family portrait courtesy of daughter, Anna T. Jarvis*

Wickersham on the bench by giving him interim appointments, largely as the result of the intervention of Birch and two other friends, Captain David H. Jarvis, Customs Collector for Alaska and a confidential advisor to the President, and Walter Clark, the Washington correspondent for *The Post-Intelligencer*. Wickersham repeatedly gave credit in his diary to these three men for their efforts on his behalf.

ALASKA SYNDICATE — 1906

W hile awaiting a decision on the appeal of the Bonanza Case, Stephen Birch continued work at the mine in the summer. In New York during the

Placer mining on Dan Creek where Stephen Birch and Dan Kain had claims. *Courtesy of Anchorage Museum of History and Art B62-1-239*

winter, he was busy lining up financial support for the construction of a railroad to reach the mine 200 miles from tidewater. During the summer of 1904, he surveyed routes for a railroad with George Hazelet, reaching the conclusion that Valdez would be the best port because building a railroad up the Copper River would not be possible. McClellan continued to work at the Bonanza Mine, and Dan Kain developed his gold placer claims on Dan Creek with financial help from Birch and his New York associates. George Howard Birch, Stephen's brother, assumed management of the Dan Creek mines in 1914 and continued to mine there until 1924 when he sold the Dan Creek Mining Company to Louis Levensaler.[14]

Placer mining on Dan Creek where Stephen Birch and Dan Kain had claims. *Courtesy of Alaska State Library, PCA159-20*

At the end of the summer of 1904, *The Alaska Prospector* in Valdez carried the following article:

> The summer season is now rapidly nearing an end and work on most of the interior properties will be shut down for the winter, the exception, however, will be the properties of the Alaska Copper Co. on the Chittyna.... the principal work performed this season was on this group in an endeavor to ascertain an approximate idea as to the tonnage it will afford as a guarantee for building a railroad. With a desire to arrive at this

estimate at as early a date as possible the work will not cease but will continue winter and summer though not as vigorously as it would were the litigation settled that is now pending on a part of the property.

The Alaska Copper Company consists of a number of very wealthy men of the East who are amply able to construct a road whenever they are reasonably sure that the tonnage of their mines will justify them in doing so. It is a cold-blooded business proposition with them and although they are now wealthy men they are not averse to being still more wealthy and with that end in view they propose to bring their holdings on the Chittyna River to a dividend paying basis at as early a date as possible.

Actually Alaska Cooper and Coal financial resources were not sufficient enough to undertake the construction of the railroad and development of the mine without help. While looking for more financial backers in 1905, Birch approached John Rosene, an entrepreneur from Nome, who already owned a railroad on the Seward Peninsula, the Northwestern Commercial Company, and the Northwestern Steamship Company. In addition, Rosene and Captain David Jarvis had just consummated a plan to purchase a number of bankrupt Alaskan canneries with financial backing from J.P. Morgan. Birch succeeded in enlisting the support of Rosene and Jarvis in his plans for a railroad from Valdez to the copper mine.[15]

Early in June 1905 Birch received the welcome news that Wickersham's ruling in the Bonanza Case had been upheld by the court of appeals. *The Alaska Prospector* announced, on July 27, 1905, that Rosene had secured financing sufficient for the first 70 miles of railroad and would soon arrive in Valdez to begin construction. On August 10, *The Alaska Prospector* carried the following article:

John Rosene of the Northwestern Steamship Co. arrived on the *Santa Clara* on Tuesday night, and Wednesday morning left town, in the company of Stephen Birch and Henry Deyo, to look over a section of the proposed railroad route. Mr. Rosene some time ago took up the proposition of building a rail-road from Valdez to the interior and has been work-ing steadily toward that end ever since. He has had a number of men in the field all summer and a large part of the survey is completed. When seen upon his arrival Mr. Rosene declined to speak as to his future actions, stating that he would be better able to declare himself upon his return from the interior, which will be in three or four days.

On September 21, *The Alaska Prospector* gave the follow-ing report:

> Work on the right-of-way through Keystone Can-yon is being carried on by a gang of men in charge of H. Deyo, for the Copper River and Northwestern Railroad Co. The rock work is progressing rapidly, and it is expected that it will be completed through the canyon in early winter.

At the same time, the paper reported that a another railroad construction crew was clearing a right-of-way for the Valdez, Copper River and Yukon Railroad Company on the other side of Keystone Canyon. Both railroad crews planned to con-tinue working during the winter according to the October 26 issue of *The Alaska Prospector*.

While Birch was enjoying success in his plans for develop-ment of the copper mine, his friend Judge Wickersham con-tinued to have problems. He returned to Washington D.C. in early 1906 in order to continue fighting for confirmation of his judicial appointment. On February 4, he recorded in his diary: "Steve Birch came over last night. He is greatly elated over getting his Bonanza Mines railroad from Valdez into shape and it now seems a success." Birch and Wickersham saw each other socially and Birch again volunteered to contact congressmen on Wickersham's behalf. On March 5, Wicker-sham wrote in the diary:

> Steve Birch came over from New York last night

and took breakfast with me this morning. He urges me to go over to New York and remain a few days as his and Mr. Ralph's friend, and I am going. He also suggests that personally he hopes I won't be confirmed as then they can employ me as the attorney for their Copper River Ry. and mining schemes.

While in New York, Birch and Wickersham called on the Morgan Bank and met W.P. Hamilton, son-in-law of J.P. Morgan, J.P. Morgan Jr. and Charles Steele .

At the end of March, Wickersham still had not been confirmed and Birch wrote offering help:

> My Dear Judge:
> I returned to New York this A.M. Mr. Ralph has informed me of the situation in Washington as best he knows.... . I saw the Morgans this morning, and they told me they had done all they possibly could for you and they felt assured you would be confirmed. Of course I don't know the situation, but my suggestion is to keep a stiff upper lip and stay in Washington. Nelson is probably trying to delay all he can. Will you kindly drop me a line as to the situation. I will necessarily be delayed here for a few days, but if you think it necessary for me to come to Washington, let me know and I will come.
> Send me word of any particular Senator that you wish to reach.[16]

Wickersham recorded in his diary that Birch contacted several senators to urge confirmation. On May 4, Wickersham wrote in the diary:

> Had dinner at New Willard with Birch tonight — he suggested that if I wished to resign next fall after they were certain about their enterprises in Alaska, they would like to have me take charge of their legal business. I told him I would be willing to make some arrangement on that line.

Several days later Wickersham visited New York and went

with Birch to meet Daniel Guggenheim, whom Wickersham refers to in his diary as "Dan Guggenheimer". Guggenheim was planning to go to Alaska to look over mining property, including Birch's copper mine. Wickersham also mentions that he met a Mr. Steele, legal counsel for the Guggenheims and brother of Charles Steele of the Morgan bank. After spending the rest of the week attending plays with Birch and James Ralph, and riding around New York in Ralph's new electric automobile, Wickersham returned to Alaska. He had still not been confirmed, but had another interim appointment from President Roosevelt .

The men that Wickersham met while in New York were the ones that Birch hoped to enlist for development of the Kennecott Mines and the access railroad. Daniel Guggenheim was already convinced, as evidenced by an interview quoted in the April 3, 1906, issue of The *New York Times*:

> Alaska is a new country. I should like to be one of those to bring it to its destined place in American affairs. It is not altogether a matter of money: there is some sentiment in an enormous undertaking of this sort.
>
> We want to go into the territory and build railroads and smelters and mining towns and bring men there and populate the country where it is habitable, and do for it what the earlier figures in American railroad building did for sections of the great West.
>
> Some of the copper districts of Alaska have already been prospected, and sections, the Copper River, for instance, have seen some development. But the mines in that country cannot be worked until railroads have put them within the reach of the seacoast and until smelters and concentrating plants are in the field to turn the ore into metal for its economical transportation to the consumer.
>
> If the plans we have made tentatively for the building of a road into the Copper River district go through the American Smelting and Refining Company will build works at some point on the coast, probably Valdez.

Guggenheim's enthusiasm was not dampened by his trip to

the North. Upon his return to New York in June 1906, he joined with the House of Morgan to form the Alaska Syndicate with the specific goal of developing Birch's copper mine. In testimony before the Senate Committee on Territories in February 1910, John N. Steele, one of the managing directors, gave the following description of the Alaska Syndicate:

> It was an agreement made in July, 1906, in the nature of a partnership, for a particular venture which they called the Alaska Syndicate. The amount of the venture was limited in that agreement to $10,000,000, but that amount could be exceeded with the consent of both parties. The particular things which were in mind at the time the Syndicate was formed were the acquisition of certain stock in the Northwestern Commercial Company, the acquisition from Mr. Rosene of the entire stock interest of the Copper River and Northwestern railway, and the acquisition from the Alaska Copper and Coal Company of an interest in the Bonanza Mine.[17]

More specifically, the Alaska Syndicate purchased 40% interest in Alaska Copper and Coal, the Copper River and Northwestern railway franchise, and 46.2% interest in the Northwestern Commercial Company, which could provide the steamships to transport ore to a smelter in Tacoma, already owned by Guggenheim interests. Stephen Birch, John N. Steele, and Silas Eccles were named managing directors of the Alaska Syndicate, with offices in New York, while John Rosene, David H. Jarvis, and William R. Rust, former owner of the Tacoma smelter, were designated as West Coast managers.

Jarvis, who had resigned from the Revenue Marine and declined Roosevelt's offer of the governorship of Alaska, had joined Rosene in developing Northwest Fisheries as a subsidiary of the Northwest Commercial Company.

RAILROAD WARFARE — 1907

Formation of the Alaska Syndicate made ample financial resources available, but also brought together a group of powerful men with differing allegiances, expertise and interests. The three New York based managing directors represented the Guggenheim interests and had the power of final approval on all development plans and expenditures. Steven Birch's agenda was the easiest to understand. He had, from the beginning, been committed to developing the copper mines. S. W. Eccles, from Utah, provided expertise in the construction and management of railroads. John Steele, not to be confused with his brother Charles Steele, an officer in the Morgan bank, was the Guggenheim attorney.

The West Coast managers were more intimately involved in the day-to-day operation of all the enterprises except the mine, which was Birch's domain. Rosene had the responsibility for railroad construction, but his primary interest was trade with Siberia . He had acquired a fleet of steamships to supply his Asian outposts, and dreamed of a rail link between Siberia and Alaska with a tunnel under the Bering Straits. Captain Jarvis, formerly an officer in the Revenue Marine, was primarily interested in fisheries and also had expertise in the management of steamships. Jarvis, who had demonstrated executive ability as head of the custom service in Alaska, was made treasurer and given proxies to vote the Morgan stock. W.R. Rust had sold his Tacoma smelting plant to Daniel Guggenheim in 1905 for $5,000,000, with the stipulation that he remain as president for at least five years at a salary of $25,000 yearly.[18]

J.P. Morgan and Daniel Guggenheim added an overall interest in the eventual industrial development of Alaska to the specific agenda of their six directors. Foreseeing the value of a readily available supply of coal for the railroad and a potential smelter, they insisted that the railroad port be close to newly discovered coal deposits in the Bering River region, several hundred miles east of Valdez. The Eastern financiers hired a railroad engineer, M.K. Rogers to study potential routes, and on July 17, 1906, *The Alaska Prospector* reported:

> If the route is found practicable the Copper River and Northwestern Railroad will move its terminus from Valdez to Catalla, on Controller bay. M.K. Rogers, representing eastern financiers interested in the road, has returned from Catalla, where he has been for six weeks with a party of twenty surveyors in the field. The route of the proposed line will be along the Catalla river, and across the Copper River, with a view to tapping the copper fields. Rogers has secured options on most of the water front property at Catalla. In an interview with John Rosene, he admitted the truth of the story. Heney, who has started a road from Orca, is here (Seattle) watching developments. He is also securing options on property at Controller bay. Both parties intend to rush construction this summer.

M.J. Heney, the contractor who built the White Pass and Yukon Railroad from Skagway to Whitehorse, had obtained a right-of-way for a railroad from Orca, the site of the current town of Cordova, up the Copper River. This route, which passed between the Miles and Childs glaciers and through narrow Abercrombie Canyon, had been surveyed by Hazelet and Birch, but deemed impassable. When Heney was unable to convince the eastern financiers to use his route, he went ahead using his own money and some from Close Brothers, the English owners of the White Pass and Yukon. Heney knew that he did not have financial resources to complete the railroad, but planned to force the Syndicate to buy him out in order to obtain his right-of-way through Abercrombie Canyon, which was too narrow to accommodate more than one railroad. The railroad from Katalla would have to pass through the canyon, so Heney threatened to set off dynamite charges if anyone entered the canyon. The threat worked. In October 1906 the Syndicate purchased Heney's Copper River Railroad for the amount he had spent plus $250,000 in Syndicate stock.

Rosene did not approve of the move to Katalla, but he was soon forced out of the Syndicate. In order to finance his projects in Siberia and the Seward Peninsula, Rosene obtained loans from the Morgan bank, using stock in Northwestern Commercial Company as collateral. He then angered Eccles by using one of the steamships in his Siberian endeavors.[19] After Rosene Jarvis and Rogers went East in late October to discuss railroad plans for the coming year, *The Alaska Prospector* reported:

Driving the first spike for Heney's Copper River Railway at Cordova, August 28, 1906. *Courtesy of Cordova Historical Society*

> On the first of the year the control of all of the Northwestern companies promoted along the coast by John Rosene will pass into the hands of the Morgan and Guggenheim interests. D.H. Jarvis will succeed Rosene in the management of the companies.

Actually Rosene continued as nominal president of Northwestern Steamship Company until the end of 1907, but lost control of the Northwestern Commercial Company.

The Syndicate was expecting great success in its railroad building efforts during the summer of 1907. The main construction crews moved to Katalla to construct a breakwater, designed by Rogers to protect the exposed shoreline. A small crew remained in Valdez to protect the Keystone Canyon rock work in case the Katalla breakwater was not successful. The Syndicate managers must have had doubts about the wisdom of the move to Katalla because they hired E.C. Hawkins, the railroad engineer who worked with Heney on the White Pass and Yukon Railway, to make a survey of the potential routes from Katalla, from Valdez, and from Cordova. Even so the Copper River and Northwestern construction crews had little reason to anticipate the difficulties they would encounter before the end of the summer.

The first problem occurred in early July at Katalla, where the Syndicate workmen were competing with another fledgling railroad. The July 27 issue of the *Fairbanks Weekly Times* reported the incident as follows:

> Under the protection of fire from detachments of armed men, a party of Guggenheim laborers succeeded in laying track over the disputed Bruner right-of-way at Catalla yesterday (July 3), but one man is dead, another may die, and nine more are seriously wounded by bullets from the Bruner blockhouses.
>
> Tony Pascal led the construction party and received the $1,000 reward offered by Guggenheim to the man who would lead the attacking forces. Soon after, he was shot dead by one of his own men, who mistook him for a member of the opposing force. ...
>
> The representative of the Bruner company here (Valdez) is making every endeavor to have the territorial government cable Washington for troops to prevent further bloodshed. In this he is backed by the residents of the town, who are sure of a continuation of hostilities.

Troops were not needed at Katalla because no further hostilities occurred. The right-of-way dispute was, instead, referred to the district court and Judge Wickersham ruled in favor of the Syndicate.

Two months later Valdez was the site of bloodshed. Hawkins had finished his assessment of the potential railroad routes, and, on September 26, 1907, the *Daily Alaska Dispatch* reported:

It is now practically decided since Engineer Hawkins filed his report that Katalla is not to be the terminus of the Guggenheim railroad to tap the Copper River copper properties of Bratnober and the Bonanza owners. On account of the expensive breakwater the terminus of the road will go to Cordova or possibly Valdez.

In anticipation of Hawkins report, George Hazelet, the Syndicate manager in Valdez, who was on a prospecting trip in the interior with Birch, was instructed to return to Valdez and prepare to start work again in Keystone Canyon. Upon arrival in

Copper River and Northwestern Railroad engine at Katalla, July 14, 1907. *Courtesy of Anchorage Museum of History and Art B89-14-41*

Valdez, Hazelet found the town in a panic. Henry Durr Reynolds, an entrepreneur with copper claims on Prince William Sound and a history of bogus mining promotions on Cook Inlet, had persuaded the citizens of Valdez to subscribe their own funds to build the Alaska Home Railway.

In order to get workmen for his railroad, Reynolds had sent M.P. Morrisey to Katalla to lure workers to Valdez with promises of liquor and money. Hazelet, anticipating trouble, hired a former deputy marshal, Edward Hasey, to guard the Syndicate rock work in Keystone Canyon and provided him with rifles. Hasey was again deputized, but, before agreeing to guard the right-of-way, exacted a promise from Hazelet that he would be backed up should trouble arise.

On the morning of September 27, after a pep rally, Morrisey led a band of his workmen, armed with picks and shovels, into Keystone Canyon. As they approached Hasey's barricade, a foreman ran out to warn them to keep away from the right-of-

Valdez citizens with the first rail for the Alaska Home Railway. *Courtesy of Alaska State Library, PCA192-17*

way. The advancing Home Railway workmen seized the Copper River and Northwestern man. Hasey warned them again by shooting in the air. When they kept on advancing, Hasey shot at their feet, wounding six. One man died later from infection in his leg wound. Hasey and Hazelet were indicted for murder, but charges against Hazelet were dropped.

Bringing in wounded from Keystone Canyon. *Courtesy of Alaska State Library, PCA192-24*

The Valdez newspaper and telegraph service were both controlled by Reynolds backers. The initial reports sent out from Valdez claimed that a group of innocent workmen had been ambushed by the Guggenheim forces, causing public opinion to be aroused against the Alaska Syndicate for using firearms to prevent competition from other railroads. In an effort to prevent riots in Valdez when it became evident several weeks later that the Home Railway promotion was not financially solvent, the Copper River and Northwestern hired back some of the Home Railway workmen, including Morrisey. Hasey was tried for murder several months later in Juneau and acquitted on the basis of the testimony of Morrisey and other Home Railway workmen. In a later trial Hasey was convicted of the lesser charge of assault with a dangerous weapon.

The Copper River and Northwestern sustained another setback in late September 1907 when violent storms washed away the Katalla breakwater. Undaunted by failures at Valdez and

Marshal Hasey's tent in Keystone Canyon. *Courtesy of Alaska State Library, PCA192-26*

Katalla, the Alaska Syndicate announced that Cordova would be the terminus of their railroad, and that Hawkins and Heney, who had succeeded in building the White Pass and Yukon, would team up again to complete the Copper River and Northwestern.

With the railroad terminus at Cordova, the Syndicate planned to build a spur line to the Bering River coal fields. However President Roosevelt, on the advice of conservationist Gifford Pinchot, had closed all potential coal fields in Alaska to entry in November 1906, and none of the 900 prospectors who had filed claims prior to the withdrawal had received patents although they paid the filing fees and did the assessment work.

Still hopeful that the stalemate would be resolved, Birch determined that the 33 claims made by a group of investors led by Clarence Cunningham had the best chance of being approved and developed to provide coal for the railroad. While Birch was busy at the mine in July 1907, Eccles completed negotiations with the Cunningham group for a half interest in the 33 claims should patents be awarded.

With access to the Bering River coal for the development of a local smelting industry in Alaska still uncertain, more ships were needed to transport ore to the Tacoma smelter. In November 1907, the Syndicate succeeded in acquiring these additional ships through a merger with the Alaska Steamship Company. The November 14 issue of the *Daily Alaska Dispatch* carried the following information:

> The Alaska Steamship Company has been taken over by the combine and merged with the Northwestern Steamship Company, the new organization to be under the management of Charles Peabody.
>
> A complete reorganization is planned involving even the removal of a number of agents... The new combine is to be handled under a management radically different from the previous one, although it is said that several of the present executive officers of the Alaska and Northwestern Steamship companies will be retained.

A week before, the same paper had announced the retirement of Rosene and the appointment of H.J. Douglas as auditor to replace M.M. Perl. The article stated that the old management had been distasteful to the Eastern men, that a new executive staff would be placed in charge, and that business would be conducted according to ideas of the big capitalists. Jarvis continued to be the treasurer and main representative of the Morgan interests, but, from the beginning, clashed with the auditor Douglas, whose allegiance was to Eccles and the Guggenheim interests.

While the Syndicate was experiencing difficulties in construction of the railroad and internal organizational upheavals, Birch forged ahead with the development of his mine. All supplies for buildings and tramways were brought by pack train over Marshall

Pass from Valdez to the Copper River, where they could be loaded on boats and carried up the Copper, Chitina and Nizina Rivers. In order to assist construction of the mine and upper reaches of the railroad before completion of the bridge between the glaciers, the steamship *Chittyna* was carried over the pass in pieces by pack

Hauling engine of river steamer *Chittyna* over Tasnuna Pass. *Courtesy of Anchorage Museum of History and Art B62-1A-126*

train during the winter of 1907. In 1907 Birch and his workmen built the general manager's office and a storehouse, and the next year they added a sawmill, bunkhouse, blacksmith shop, and the Bonanza tramway terminal. When railroad tracks reached Aber-

Unloading S.S *Nizina* at upriver railroad camp. *Courtesy of Washington State Historical Society—Curtis Collection*

crombie Landing on the lake in front of Miles Glacier, Birch was able to send ore samples by boat to meet trains that carried them to the port at Cordova. Foreseeing the eventual need for a settlement at the junction of the Copper and Chitina Rivers, Birch homesteaded a site for the town of Chitina in 1908.

FRONTIER POLITICS — 1908

Although Stephen Birch was moving ahead on development of the mine, he was encountering problems in persuading associates to employ his friend Judge Wickersham as an attorney for the Alaska Syndicate. Had he been more successful, the next several years would have been more pleasant for the Syndicate and the history of Alaska might have been profoundly altered. In an April 8, 1907 letter to Wickersham, Birch explained that other members of the Syndicate had different legal commitments:

> The consolidation of the Alaska S.S. Co. and the Northwestern S.S. Co. will not go through, any how for the present. Peabody wants too much cash. We are all good friends however and will work in harmony. I do not think this will interfere with my plans about employing general counsel but it will be necessary for me to work on our people in N.Y. Young Mr. Morgan has instructed Jarvis and Rosene to employ the law firm that young Spooner is in, so you can see where the work will have to be done.
>
> We expect to leave here on the 10th and should be in N.Y. on the 25th. Will advise you soon as possible. Spooner wants to make a yearly arrangement, but I have told Jarvis to hold him off. Will see you about June first.[20]

On June 3, Birch further explained the status in a letter to Wickersham:

The situation is not clear as I would want it. As I wrote you some time ago, we did not purchase the Peabody line, and as a result the N.W. Commercial Co. is still managed about the same as in the past. Hartman has been acting as attorney for the N.W. Co. and Bogle for the R.R. Co.

The Morgans had because of Spooner practically engaged Bogle for this year, and am looking up the minutes of the N.W. Co. Found that Hartman had been engaged for another year at six thousand dollars per year. Bogle has not a fixed fee, so I guess the attorney bills will be large enough by the end of the year to show good reason for a General Counsel.

I talked with all my people and they would like to have you, so I hope you plan so that you and I can get together with our people this fall and settle the matter before it comes time to renew the arrangements with Bogle and Hartman.

Governor Wilfred Hoggatt with Michael J. Heney, Copper River and Northwestern Railroad Contractor. *Courtesy of Washington State Historical Society—Curtis Collection*

Am sorry we cannot have a talk now. It is so much more satisfactory than writing. ... I want you with us and, if you will help me, can do the trick. I leave tomorrow on the *Saratoga* for Katalla, and expect to go inside all summer.

Saw Gov. Hoggatt. He says you are very busy. Trusting you are well.[21]

Wickersham and Alaska's territorial governor, Wilfred Hoggatt, had been good friends until June 1907 when Wickersham refused to disbar a young Juneau attorney who had offended Hoggatt. On July 1, Wickersham expressed this antagonism to Hoggatt in his diary:

> Well. Gov. Hoggatt, Shackleford and others of their — and my — friends are tearing their hair and rending their garments because I did not disbar Cobb. They have involved Marshal Shoup in the matter and have distressed him greatly with their mutterings.
>
> I am as greatly disappointed as they are, for I expected decent treatment from them and did not get it. Well, they can go to the devil. I never have tempered my legal duties to suit either friends or enemies and don't intend to do so.
>
> Finis. Governor!

Hoggatt was equally strong in his reaction to the episode. On September 13 he sent letters to both President Roosevelt and Secretary of the Interior James Garfield advising against "the longer continuance of Judge Wickersham on the bench."[22] These letters from Hoggatt were partially responsible for Wickersham's decision to resign from the bench and enter private law practice in Fairbanks. Birch responded on November 15, 1907 from New York to the news of Wickersham's resignation, and reiterated his desire to employ Wickersham:

> Dear Judge:
>
> Your letter of October the 3rd, written from Fairbanks, received. Also copies of communications which have passed between yourself and others in re Alaska Home Railway Co., and I thank you for the same. I regret very much indeed that there should have arisen any unpleasantness between yourself and the Governor. I do not know all the circumstances, but think I realize how you feel, and while I am sorry that you resigned without having it understood who was to be your successor, I nevertheless feel that it is better for your own personal interest to

resign from office. I am fond of Hoggatt and know that he is headstrong, but am surprised that he should undertake to interfere or take exception to your decision. I have not seen Hoggatt, but understand from others that he was disappointed with your decision. I thought Hoggatt was too big a man to be spiteful. I note that you are going to stay in Fairbanks until spring and practice law, and hope by the time you get out that the Seattle Companies will be in a position to avail themselves of your services. No change has been made other than what I wrote you last spring. Bogle is the attorney for the Company.

I leave here tomorrow for Seattle, expecting to remain there several months. I hope it can be brought about so that our people can make you a satisfactory proposition.[23]

Wickersham responded from Fairbanks on December 19, 1907, providing Birch with some indication of future plans:

My Dear Birch:

I am in receipt of your kind letter of November 15, from New York, saying that you are coming out to Seattle to remain several months. I was very glad to hear from you and pleased to know through the newspapers that your enterprise at Cordova is under way. I regret, however, to notice that the price of copper has taken a slump but I sincerely hope that by the time you are ready to sell some that the price will be soaring again. ...

I am going to practice law as soon as the new judge gets here, though when that will be the Lord only knows. ... I am getting very nervous about the delay, and anxious to get out of office. Just as Captain Jarvis wrote to me, the actual effort to get out when I got up courage enough to do so, was nothing at all when compared to what it seemed to be and now that the effort has been made and my resignation accepted I am anxious for my successor to get here so that I may take up the effort to make some money. I am going to forget my enemies, even if I don't forgive them. I am not going to try to get even with anybody but I am going to work.[24]

On February 1, 1908, Wickersham again wrote Birch an update on his plans, and indicated continued interest in the copper development:

> I entered upon the practice of law the first of January and I think I am going to succeed in making some money. ...
>
> I do not want you to let me drop entirely out of your thoughts, now that I have become a common citizen, but write to me once in a while and give me the latest situation. I am always greatly interested in your success and I try to keep posted in relation to transportation matters and railway building in the neighborhood of the Copper River.[25]

Since Wickersham was now in private practice and potentially available for hire, Birch hoped to push for his employment at the next annual meeting of the Syndicate in Seattle . On March 17, 1908, he wrote Wickersham:

> Dear Judge:
>
> I still call you Judge, and expect that name will remain with you for the rest of your days although you do not now hold that office. ...
>
> Expect to be in Seattle the latter part of April. Do you expect to be out this spring? I wish you would advise me as to what your future plans are. If you are going to be out, I should like very much to have you meet Mr. Eccles, who will also be in Seattle at the same time I am there. Will probably return to New York again before going to Alaska for the summer
>
> Mr. Bogle is still the General Counsel for the Northwestern Commercial Company and subsidiaries. Whether he will be General Counsel after the annual meeting I cannot say at this time. My

people are beginning to realize that the Company should have a General Counsel whose entire time shall be given up to them. If I can get them to take action at the annual meeting, a change might be made. I wish you could advise me, and address me care of Northwestern Commercial Company, Lowman Building, Seattle, if you would care to become the General Counsel for the Company in Seattle, and what compensation you would wish. Please address me personally. If you do not care to come to Seattle, will you let me know what your plans are, and where you are going to make your headquarters.[26]

Wickersham answered promptly from Fairbanks on April 8, 1908, expressing his interest in employment by the Syndicate:

My Dear Mr. Birch:
Your letter of March 17th has been received and I hasten my answer that it may catch the last mail out over the ice.

I regret that I cannot meet you in Seattle the latter part of the month, because one can make one's ideas plainer in conversation than by writing, but since the opening of the April term of courts prevents it, I shall briefly state the matter by letter.

I have entered upon the practice of law here, and represent some of the most important interests in the territory, and the outlook for returns is satisfactory, still I long for the flesh pots of the "outside", and would accept an offer from your allied Alaska interests to act as their General Counsel, but not in any subordinate capacity. I will accept a three years contract at $15,000 per annum with offices in Seattle and office force and maintenance. Upon that sort of arrangement I would devote my time exclusively to their interests, and give them the best service possible. My opportunities here, however, are so good that I could not afford to give them up for less than a three years contract with you. Please advise me by

wire if anything is done in connection with this offer
and it may be thus arranged.

Remember me kindly to Captain Jarvis.[27]

Wickersham's letter, however, did not reach Birch prior to
the meeting at which Eccles was elected president and Jarvis
secretary-treasurer. Birch wrote Wickersham on May 6, 1908
from New York, on stationary that reflected the new name,
Kennecott Mines Company. In this letter Birch indicates that
S.W. Eccles had become the dominant force in the Syndicate,
but that he still had control over the mine business.

Dear Judge:

Your letters of December 19th, 1907 and April 8th,
1908, have been forwarded to me here in New York.

I note that your letter of December 19th was returned to you because of want of local address. You
are right, I am of very little noise in Seattle, and wish
I was less in other places. ...

Regarding your letter of April 8th, in answer to
my letter of March 17th, I was sorry indeed not to
have seen you in Seattle . I thought from your previous letter that you were coming out anyhow to Seattle, and wanted you to meet Mr. Eccles, President
of the Copper River and Northwestern Railway, and
the leading spirit in the Guggenheim-Morgan Syndicate . I did not even receive your letter in Seattle, it
was forwarded to me here in New York with the
other mail. We held the annual meetings and the
firm of Bogle and Spencer were employed as General Counsel for the Railroad and Commercial Company at a salary of $1,000 per month. The Kennecott
Mines Company have not joined in this, nor will they
do so. Bogle seems to have been giving satisfaction
to the Morgan people, and old man Spooner has
been pulling for the Bogle and Spooner firm with
the Morgan people.

In a talk I had with Jarvis regarding you, he suggested that you become one of the firm of Bogle
and Spooner, and stated to me that he had some talk

with you in regard to this, but since receiving your letter I do not think that this would be satisfactory to you. You are right in wanting a contract of at least three years, for I am satisfied that you can make as much as you mentioned in Alaska, if not more. I really think that there are greater opportunities in Alaska than there would be in devoting your entire time to the allied interests of the Alaska Syndicate in Seattle . When I wrote to you I wanted your own ideas regarding this proposition, so that I could be in position to bring you in touch with Mr. Eccles, provided you wished me to do so. Now my conclusion, Judge, is this, personally, I want to do for you that which is the best for your interest, and after reviewing the entire situation, believe that at this time the General Counselship of the Alaska Syndicate has not as good a future in it, nor the opportunity of making money, as a free lance like yourself will have in Alaska.

Faithfully yours, Stephen Birch.[28]

On May 11, 1908, Birch again wrote Wickersham from New York, implying his continued interest in making some arrangement for legal employment:

Am sorry indeed that I did not see you in Seattle, for the interest of our concern I am sorry also that you are not at this time connected with them, although my own personal opinion is that you will make more money in Alaska. However I want to have a talk with you on this whole matter. Bogel has not been employed for any definite period. His firm simply looks after the business of the Railroad Company at a monthly salary.[29]

These letters apparently took a long time in reaching Wickersham because he did not record his reaction in the diary until July 8:

Received letter from Stephen Birch about his de-

sires that I be employed as the general counsel for
the N.W. Ry. and Steamship Co. and the Guggenheim-
Morgan exploiters of copper in Alaska. Nothing done
yet and I am satisfied that nothing can be. He tells me
that Bogle and Spooner are serving the company for
$1,000 per month — I asked $15,000 a year! I am glad
I did ask that amount. Things may come around in
time so that I can assist Birch — but I am not inclined
to hurry the situation for I can make more money as
I am. My business here is good and it will bring me as
much or more than that Co. pays B.& S. at Seattle and
I am, as Birch says, a free lance!

We can only speculate whether the outcome might have
been different had the directors of the Alaska Syndicate received Wickersham's proposal for employment prior to their
annual meeting. As it happened, Wickersham had already
made a momentous decision regarding his own future when
he received Birch's letters explaining the lack of response to
his terms for employment by the Syndicate. On June 23, 1908,
Wickersham telegraphed Jarvis in Seattle : "I intend to run for
Congress. Where is Birch?" Jarvis immediately wired back:
"Birch in New York. Leaves tomorrow. Due here July first.
Don't you think little late?" Jarvis followed up the telegram
with a letter in which he stated that, although he was not a
voting resident of Alaska, he had already stated support of
the regular Republican candidate, John W. Corson. He also
cautioned Wickersham about the possible danger to his political future of breaking with the Republican party.[30]

When Birch reached Seattle and learned of Wickersham's
proposed candidacy for delegate, he responded on July 6:

Dear Judge:
Have just returned to Seattle from the east and
expect to leave here on the 8th for Cordova to go in
to the interior for the summer. Capt. Jarvis showed
me your telegram stating that you intended to run
for Congress and asking where I was.
Capt. Jarvis seems to be of the opinion, and I feel
the same, that we would have liked very much in-

deed to have had you announce your candidacy before the Republican convention was held in Alaska and before Corson was nominated, and believe you would have received the nomination had you wished it and would have received the strongest support. It is unfortunate that the distance is so great that we cannot keep better in touch with one another so that we could know what was going on. It does seem to me as being late for you to announce your candidacy. I had no idea that you cared for any more political positions and was somewhat surprised to hear that you had decided to again get into politics.

Am very sorry indeed that there should be any misunderstanding between Governor Hoggatt and yourself. Personally I desire harmony and think for the best interests of Alaska and for all her good citizens that the least strife we have amongst ourselves the better.

It seems to me that if you should lay low this election and come out strong in advance of the next election and run on the Republican ticket that you could win out very easily.

Of course, Judge, I do not wish to assume to dictate what your actions shall be but only wish to convey to you my own impressions. I wish to be your friend and want you to consider me as such and hope you will take my suggestions in the spirit in which they are offered.[31]

Wickersham was more concerned with his political future than with the friendship of Birch or Jarvis. Since it was apparent that he would not receive their endorsement for his candidacy, he looked elsewhere for political support. Upon receipt of the Jarvis letter on July 17, 1908, Wickersham wrote in his diary:

Letter from Jarvis, Mgr. of the Guggenheims from Seattle and he strongly advised me to keep out of the race and announced his intention to support Corson. Immediately revised my address — then almost done and put in a strong plank against Guggenheim domination in mining and transportation matters in Alaska.

This was Wickersham's first mention of any opposition to the Alaska Syndicate, but from then on he made every effort possible to renounce any connection with his former friends, Jarvis and Birch. Wickersham realized that public opinion in Alaska still blamed the Alaska Syndicate for the bloodshed at Keystone Canyon, and that independent Alaskan miners feared domination by Eastern financiers. The Democratic candidate tried to point out that, in fact, Wickersham had always been friendly to the Guggenheim interests, which indeed had been the case up to that point. Jarvis tried to see Wickersham several days before the August election, and Wickersham wrote in his diary:

> Capt. Jarvis came in this afternoon on the *Northwestern* and has been trying to see me, but I have purposely avoided him — he is the Pacific coast manager of the Guggenheim interests — and since I am loudly called a Guggenheim man, I am at a loss to understand his action. He can not assist me — he can only do me an injury by even inquiring for me and exhibiting an interest in my presence here. I will not permit him to assist my candidacy and I hesitate to act discourteously toward him. I wish he would leave me alone.

Wickersham understood the reasoning of the typical Alaskan voter. His anti-Guggenheim campaign paid off. He was elected delegate to Congress on August 11, 1908 despite M.J. Heney's attempts to get out the Corson vote in Cordova by transporting railway workers to the polls on special trains.

In spite of Wickersham's attacks on the Syndicate's Alaska operations, Birch still attempted to preserve his friendship with the new delegate. On September 9, 1908, he wrote Wickersham from his office at the Kennecott Mines:

> My Dear Judge:
> Am advised that you have been elected Delegate,

and wish to congratulate you on you election. It takes some time for news to get in here, hence this delay in sending my congratulations.

As I wrote you from Seattle, I was surprised to hear that you again desired public office, although a few days after receiving your telegram, was again advised that you had withdrawn; later on that you had again come into the race. While I do not know Corson personally, I had been advised by men whom

"HIS MASTER'S VOICE."

Political cartoon from the *Fairbanks Daily Times*, July 6, 1908.

I considered your friends that he was all right, and the Governor pledged my support last June, which, as a matter of fact amounts to very little, and as you know, I am not a very popular man in politics myself. I was further advised that you would make a

mistake to run at this time, as an independent candidate would complicate matters. However, your election shows that I have been ill advised, and am really glad that it is so, and hope that when you go to
Washington all this wrangling over Alaska Legisla-
tion will be stopped, and that we can all expect more
harmony in the future.

Wishing you success, and trusting that you will
look me up when you come east, I am very faithfully yours, Stephen Birch.[32]

Upon receipt of this letter, Wickersham wrote in his diary
on October 16, 1908:

This letter gives me a chance to give Birch and his
crowd a good `roast' and I sure intend to do it, and
try and get them to break away from the Governor
in Territorial politics.

When Wickersham went to Washington in 1909, the feud
with Governor Hoggatt continued. Wickersham insisted that
Hoggatt was acting as a lobbyist for the Guggenheims and
demanded that Richard A. Ballinger, the new Secretary of the
Interior in William Howard Taft's administration, order Hoggatt to leave Washington and return to Alaska. Wickersham
and Birch continued to correspond, primarily about some
gold mining claims that Wickersham hoped to interest the
Guggenheims in developing. On March 26, 1909, Wickersham
wrote in his diary:

Have had a long consultation with Stephen Birch,
Eccles and Steele of the Copper River Ry. Co. this
afternoon, and I told them with brutal frankness about
the Cordova election frauds, the fight their people
made against me in the last election. They listened
with interest. I explained that I wanted a law passed
giving Alaska a local legislature and that I wanted
them to help me and that I wanted Gov. Hoggatt to
go home and attend to his duties as governor, etc.
The conversation covered the conditions in Alaska

very fully and I think some good will come of it. I explained very frankly to them that I only asked fair consideration for the people of Alaska and wanted nothing from them politically. That their support politically would do me more harm than good, etc.

Governor Hoggatt resigned in May 1909, and President Taft appointed Walter Clark, the newspaper correspondant who had worked hard in support of Wickersham judicial confirmation, partly in the hope that this would heal the feud between Alaska's delegate and governor. Rather than being pleased, Wickersham was offended that his advice had not been sought. In his diary he referred to Clark as a "subservient servant of Jarvis, the Guggenheim Trust, etc.," but decided against actively opposing the appointment. Clark left Washington and spent all of his time attending to gubernatorial duties in Juneau. Peace reigned in Alaska politics for a brief time.

MUCKRAKING — 1910

The summer of 1909 was a peaceful and productive one for Birch and the Alaska Syndicate. With Governor Clark minding his business in Juneau, Wickersham suspended his attacks on the Guggenheims and set to work preparing a bill to provide Alaska with an elected legislature. Hawkins and Heney took charge of the railroad project and work on the Copper River and Northwestern was finally progressing satisfactorily, although the railroad would not be completed in time to meet a deadline set by Birch and his original backers. In order to protect their 40% interest in the mines, the Alaska Syndicate purchased the remaining 60% from Alaska Copper and Coal for $3,000,000, retaining Birch as manager.

In the anticipation of being able to ship copper ore out over the railroad, Birch assembled an able core of assistants to run the mines. Lewis Levensaler left the Anaconda company and went to work for Birch in 1908, first mapping the gold placer claims at Dan Creek, and then going to Kennecott in 1909 to prepare the Bonanza and Jumbo for mining. Later that year Birch sent Levensaler to LaTouche Island in Prince William Sound to survey and sample the Beatson Mine. Levensaler forwarded his data to Birch in New York, and in 1910 Birch purchased the Beatson Mine.

The New York financiers sent more mining and transportation experts to look over their Alaska projects in 1909. Pope Yeatman, who assessed the mines for the Guggenheims, was favorably impressed and confirmed previous optimistic reports. The Morgans sent A.H. Gray to look over the railroad situation. While Gray and Birch were touring Alaska looking for a feasible route extension to the Tanana Valley, they met with Falcon Joslin and Martin Harrais. At this meeting Birch said that J.P. Morgan had given him the following instructions: "Steve, when you go into that Tanana country, I want you to pay particular attention to the agricultural possibilities. If they can raise stuff like that man Joslin brought out two years ago, and those pioneers want to stay there after the gold is mined out, I'll build a railroad in there for them. I don't care a damn what it costs me, or whether I get a cent of the investment back! I'd like to help those pioneers, who had the courage to go in there. I'd like to make it possible for them to remain. John D. Rockefeller has built

Officials of Alaska Syndicate meeting on board the S.S. *Yucatan* in July 1908. Stephen Birch, 5th from right; Michael Heney, 4th from right; George Hazelet, 8th from right. *Courtesy of Washington State Historical Society—Curtis Collection*

churches and Andrew Carnegie, libraries, as their monuments — I am going to build a railroad to benefit those Alaska pioneers as my monument!" [33]

Birch contacted Wickersham in Fairbanks during one of these trips and spent time photographing gardens, perhaps to reassure J.P. Morgan about the agricultural potential of the Tanana Valley. Wickersham also took Birch to see some of his own mining prospects, and reported in his diary on August 3, 1909:

Birch is not strongly impressed with the quartz

showings on Cleary. He says, and I think correctly, that it is a "good prospect", but not a mine. He also said to me (privately) that it was too small for his people to invest in, and I think nothing can be done about selling these mines before more extensive work is done in developing the same.

The entire country was optimistic about Alaska's development possibilities during the summer of 1909. Huge crowds were attending the Alaska-Yukon Exposition in Seattle and learning that the great Northern territory was ready for settlement. Richard Ballinger, the new Secretary of the Interior was a Westerner from Seattle and far more receptive to development than his conservationist predecessor, James Garfield. There was even hope that, with Ballinger in the Interior Department, the coal fields in Alaska might finally be opened. When President Taft visited the Exposition in September to speak on his plans for Alaska, many people expected that he would advocate more self-government for the territory. Instead he proposed a military commission government, similar to one that he had set up as governor of the Phillipines. This attitude on the part of the Taft administration did not bode well for Wickersham's bill to create an elected legislature in Alaska and suggested trouble ahead.

Trouble started on November 13, 1909, when *Collier's Weekly* carried a front page story with the headline: "The Whitewashing of Ballinger: Are the Guggenheims in Charge of the Interior Department." This article was the culmination of a feud between Ballinger and Gifford Pinchot, head of the National Forests in the Department of Agriculture. Pinchot was upset that Taft had not retained Garfield as head of the Interior Department. Ballinger was amenable to transferring land to private interests for development, while Pinchot wished to keep more federal land in reservations. When Pinchot found out that Ballinger had tentatively cleared the Cunningham claims in the Bering River coal field for patents, he thought he might have a way of getting rid of Ballinger. Since the Alaska Syndicate had taken an option on a half interest in the Cunningham claims, he planned to invoke the specter of the dreaded Guggenheims, accusing them of trying to control the

Taft administration. The muckraking press printed deroga-
tory articles about Ballinger that prompted him to sue *Collier's*
for libel. The feud drew so much public attention that Congress decided to hold a special investigation of both the Interior and Agricultural Departments.

Just as the Pinchot-Ballinger hearings were about to start in
Washington, President Taft arranged to have Senator Beveridge
introduce a bill to create the military-style commission to gov-
ern Alaska. This bill was in direct opposition to the bill that
would create an elected legislature. Wickersham was furious.
To make matters worse, he was barred from attending hear-

Captain D.H. Jarvis reading *Colliers* magazine article. *Courtesy of Mary Jarvis Cocke, granddaughter of David Jarvis*

ings on the bill before the Committee on Territories. The del-
egate reacted by accusing everyone who favored the Beveridge
Bill, including Major Wilds Richardson, head of the Alaska
Road Commission, of being controlled by the Guggenheims.

Wickersham found another way to fight back, as revealed
by the January 16, 1910 entry in his diary:

> Today, however, a ray of hope comes from a
> visit which I received from Mr. Ben B. Hampton,
> the owner and proprietor of *Hampton's Magazine*.
> This is one of the great magazines of New York —
> a muckraker of the most virulent type —a fighter

of Apacheland, and one which can reach millions of readers. ... I gave them facts and exhibited evidence in my possession and told them how more could be obtained — and, in short, an arrangement was entered into that Mr. Lyle, for *Hampton*, is to begin the story at once and *Hampton's Magazine* will immediately enter upon a campaign of indictment, arraignment, and trial of the Administration's scheme of a Guggenheim Commission government for Alaska. I see no other way to fight it, and they are anxious and willing to take up the fight, and I expressed a perfect willingness to assist them. So the Battle for a government by the People in Alaska is on and I may no longer hope for any thing from the Administration but War — but thank God I will now be able to reach an audience — the Public, and the Echo will get into Congress even if my voice cannot.

For myself, I shall be as discrete as I can — smile and be a still villain until the Administration shall find out that I am furnishing the facts — evidence— and then I'll fight openly. We begin the War tomorrow and I am delighted. I do not anticipate an easy victory — maybe not a victory at all — but as to that one takes the chances in War, and I can no longer refuse the risk — and will go armed with the spear and javelin for whatever enemy appears.

The facts that Wickersham presented to the magazine and to the Committee on Territories were calculated to exaggerate the influence of the Alaska Syndicate. For example, he accused the Syndicate of trying to control the Bering River coal field, when, in truth they had only an option, that was never exercised, on 33 out of 900 claims. He also claimed that the Syndicate controlled the White Pass and Yukon Railroad, when the only connection was a small amount of Syndicate stock given to Samuel Graves of Close Brothers when the Syndicate bought Heney's fledgling Copper River Railroad in 1906.

In mid-February, Stephen Birch and John N. Steele asked to

testify at hearings before the Committee on Territories and tell the true story of the Syndicate's Alaska activities. The testimony, given by Birch with Steele acting as the questioning attorney, was simple and factual in all respects. Wickersham's reaction was shown by his diary entry on February 18, 1910:

Birch is before the Senate Committee on Territo-

Cartoon published during Pinchot-Ballinger controversy in 1910.
Courtesy of Washington State Historical Society—Curtis Collection

ries today — he and Steele have slid in quietly and gave testimony to show that the Guggenheims are real good people and do not own Alaska and its resources. Of course their statements are prepared to minimize their efforts in Alaska — and they gave me no notice. I did not find it out until they had finished, but I intend to be present tomorrow morning when they are to be cross examined.

The following day Wickersham did attend the hearings, but was told that he could not cross examine Birch. That day he wrote in his diary:

> At the last of his testimony, Birch did a very untruthful and ungentlemanly thing in saying that I had — after I was no longer on the bench and before I was elected delegate — applied to them for employment as attorney, but that I had not been retained. I then said to the Com. that Mr. Birch had stated the fact unfairly since the truth was that he wrote me a letter suggesting my employment and then I read to the Com. from my letter press copybook the three or four paragraphs saying that in answer to his letter I would accept employment if it was desired by them. Beveridge was a mean and cunning as a fox in his efforts to injure me and to put me in a false light, but I got it straight — thanks to Senator Hughes of Colorado.
>
> Their refusal to permit a cross examination of Birch and Steele ought to create a decided impression against the Guggenheims and anything the Beveridge Committee may do in their aid and assistance.

One part of Birch's testimony that aroused nationwide interest was his estimation of the possible worth of the coal in the Bering River coal fields. Experts, such as Arthur H. Brooks of the United States Geological Survey corroborated Birch's estimates of the mineral wealth of Alaska. This emphasis on the mineral wealth of Alaska, coupled with Wickersham's exaggerated accounts of the Alaska Syndicate holdings, only served to increase the nationwide suspicion of the Guggenheims.

The next month Birch and Steele appeared before the Pinchot-Ballinger hearings at their own request in order to refute statements made to the press by Wickersham in which he claimed that the Guggenheims "owned all the fishes, the mines, the railroads, the steamship lines, and the rivers —all of Alaska." Steele testified as follows:

> We ought to have encouragement in the building of our Copper river railroad. It is the only enterprise of its kind in that country.
>
> Now as to the Wickersham charges — he said we own all the fish — well, we only have $300,000 worth out of about $3,000,000, which is the total production. We only own 12 out of 28 of the steamers running to Alaska; we own one railroad, and have no coal, nor interest in any claims except the Cunningham group.
>
> We want equal rights under the law with all others in developing the country. We have never attempted to shut out any others or tried to stifle competition. We ought to receive any encouragement Congress can give us.

Articles began appearing in the April issue of *Hampton's Magazine* and other muckraking magazines, distorting Birch's testimony and amplifying Wickersham's claims of Syndicate domination. On April 30, Wickersham received a surprise visit from Birch, which he described in his diary:

> I was greatly surprised this morning when Stephen Birch, the managing director of the Alaska Syndicate called me up at breakfast and wanted to see me. He came to my office at 9:30 and remained till 12, and then went over with me to the New Varnum and took dinner with Debbie and me. ... Birch begged me to quit the fight and to give them terms of peace. He said "What do you want us to do? We will do anything you say. Just say it, and it will be done, etc. He wanted the fight against them stopped — but I said, "Can you stop a prairie fire when the whole great grassy plain is ablaze and driven before a 50-mile gale?" I denounced their Cordova paper, the stuffing of the Cordova ballot

box, the fixing of the Valdez grand jury and the bribery of the Deputy District Attorney and then showed him the Douglas copies of John A. Carson's letter to Jarvis, and the accompanying account, when the bribery of jurors and witnesses in the Hasey case was admitted, and approved by Bogle and paid by Jarvis. He certainly was perturbed by these photographic copies of their criminality, and begged me to quit. Plainly I told him I would when his people would quit their criminal practices and support my efforts to give a popular legislative government to Alaska. He went away unhappy, and I then filed my letters and charges including a copy of the two photographic exhibits with the Senate Committee and Judiciary. ...

I may be defeated finally on my fight against the Taft appointive military legislative bill, but they will know that Alaska has a Delegate at any rate.

This diary entry refers to another Wickersham plan to force the Taft administration to support his bill for an elected legislature. Several months before, H.J. Douglas, a former auditor for the Alaska Syndicate in Seattle whom Jarvis had fired, approached Wickersham with two documents that he had removed from the files in the hope that he could use them against Jarvis. The papers consisted of a letter from John A. Carson, an attorney in the first Hasey trial, to Jarvis explaining a bill from M.P. Morrisey for the lodging and feeding of some of the witnesses during the trial. Carson's letter explained that Morrisey had been helpful in "taking care of some of the witnesses", which could be interpreted in a number of different ways. Wickersham sent copies of these papers to the Attorney General with a demand that both Jarvis and Carson be prosecuted and planned to claim that the Justice Department was controlled by the Guggenheims if the prosecution was not promptly undertaken.

When investigation by the Attorney General failed to reveal definite evidence of witness and jury tampering in the Hasey case, Wickersham got Douglas to swear an affidavit that Jarvis had once been party to cheating the government out of $6,700 through collusive bidding on a coal contract. Wickersham then demanded that the Attorney General prosecute Jarvis on this charge, implying that any failure to do so would prove that the Justice Department was controlled by the Guggenheims. The nationwide press coverage of these accusations so depressed Jarvis, to whom honor and a good name were all important, that he committed suicide of June 23, 1911.

Birch had no direct contact with Wickersham after the meeting in April 1910. Occasionally they communicated indirectly through an intermediary, such as Falcon Joslin, and Birch took precautions not to interfere with Wickersham politically. On January 29. 1911, Wickersham wrote in his diary: "Saw Stephen Birch and Mr. Ralph in the Waldorf dining room, but did not go near them and did not speak."

Wickersham did succeed in killing the Beveridge Bill, and Alaska got an elected legislature with little real political power. All the claims in the Bering River coal fields were cancelled and the coal there has never been mined. The negative publicity that the Guggenheims and Morgans received as a result of the Pinchot-Ballinger hearings and Wickersham's "war" effectively cancelled any plans to extend the Copper River and Northwestern Railroad beyond Chitina and the Kennecott Mines. M.J. Heney died before the railroad was completed, but Eccles and Hawkins drove the "copper spike" at Kennecott on March 29, 1911. Birch had a load of copper ore ready to go. He had fulfilled his part of the bargain and the Kennecott Mine was in production.

KENNECOTT CORPORATION — 1915

In order to live up to his promise to have ore ready for shipment when the railroad was completed, Stephen Birch had to install a 15,000 foot aerial tramway to the Bonanza Mine, 4,500 feet above the railroad terminal. All materials for this tramway, in addition to cars, rails, and provisions for both people and horses, were sledded 225 miles from Valdez

The Bonanza tramway. *Courtesy of Anchorage Museum of History and Art B72-32-223*

during the winter under the capable direction of R.H. McClellan.[34] McClellan, one of the initial locators, also supervised the logging and sawmill operation. Soon after completion of the railroad, Birch planned construction of a concentrating mill. About 25,000 tons of crude ore, shipped to the Tacoma smelter before the mill was completed, returned 72 percent copper and 18 oz. of silver per ton, justifying this further expenditure, although financiers had already invested 30 million dollars on the mining property, steamship line and railroad without any return.

Birch expressed frustration with the coal situation to a reporter from the *Seattle Times* in June, 1911, while enroute to Alaska to supervise the installation of the large crushing mill and concentrating plant at the Bonanza Mine:

> We have hoped against hope that the Alaska coal fields would be opened so that we could be saved the cost of transporting fuel a distance of nearly 1500 miles, but this has seemed impossible of accomplishment, and the Alaska coal situation has ceased to be of interest to the Alaska Syndicate.

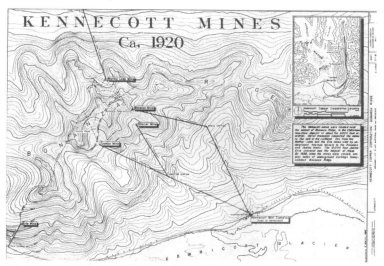

Courtesy of Historical American Engineering Record National Parks Service—Delineated by E. Martin. 1986

> Under the belief that the government could not keep the coal lands tied up, the Syndicate expended a good many millions of dollars in opening up the Bonanza copper mines and in building a railroad to open up the Copper River valley and the ore bodies contiguous thereto. There is not a railroad in the United States that could make a profit if paying $10 a ton for coal.
>
> The proposition figures out that we can get the equivalent of one ton of coal in crude oil at a cost of $3.50.

Alaskan coal would be even cheaper. But the saving effected as between coal and oil is sufficient to cut quite a considerable figure in the cost of production of copper.

With ore shipments from the Bonanza Mine leaving Kennecott twice weekly, Birch began to develop the Jumbo claim, two miles northwest of Bonanza, with a second complete tramway to the mill. The Jumbo tramway was completed in 1913 and the capacity of the mill increased to 500 tons per day. H. DeWitt Smith, who became foreman of the Bonanza Mine in February 1914, described the status of the mine when he first arrived at Kennecott:

> Copper production of ten to twelve million pounds per annum was maintained from the Bonanza and Jumbo mines by milling 700 tons per day, with the mill shut down in the winter months due to water shortage. Mine operations had reached a depth of only 600 feet below the adit levels, and ore tonnage was maintained by hauling one-ton ships up 30-degree incline shafts, with 50 to 75 HP electric single-drum hoists. Ore was transported from each mine by aerial tramway to the mill, 4500 feet lower in elevation than the mines. Sorted high-grade ore and concentrates were sacked for rail and water shipment to Tacoma, with rail traffic to Cordova interrupted for four to six weeks during spring breakup, with the yearly washing out of the wooden bridge over the Chitina River. The expenditure for bridge reconstruction represented a much lower cash outlay than the interest on the cost of a permanent steel structure. This was a nice little mine operation, which could not possibly repay the amounts expended by the Alaska Syndicate.[35]

Prospects for cash return from the mines began to look brighter in the summer of 1914 when a rich chalcocite body, which yielded up to 70 percent copper ore without sorting or concentration, was encountered on the Jumbo 500-foot level. The following year, the Alaska Syndicate decided to offer stock in the Alaska mines to the public. On April 29, 1915, the Kennecott Company was incorporated, retaining the misspelling of the name of the nearby Kennicott Glacier, named after the explorer Robert Kennicott. In regard to this spelling, Levensaler commented: "Who changed the spelling to Kennecott, I don't know, perhaps Stephen Birch, who did not know any better."[36] Birch became president of the new corporation, which purchased the Kennecott Mines Company and Beatson Copper Company for 720,000 shares of stock, plus $10,000,000 in 6 percent bonds convertible into 400,000 more Kennecott Copper shares. William P. Hamilton, Silas Eccles, and John Steele, all former Alaska Syndicate officers, were listed among the directors, as was H.O. Havemeyer.

The following summer, Birch engaged Henry Krumb, a well-known consulting engineer from Salt Lake City, to examine and value the Alaska properties. Smith, who was present at the time, reported Krumb's advice to Birch:

> Mr. Krumb raised the point with Mr. Birch one day,

Kennecott Mine. *1918 Courtesy of Anchorage Museum of History and Art B72-32-16*

> while sitting on the Jumbo high-grade ore dump, of the uncertainty in length of life of the Kennecott properties, and that rather than pay total dividends of forty to fifty million dollars over the next several years and then drop down to a much lower rate, it would be preferable to initiate a modest dividend rate and use the balance of earnings to make a substantial investment in some property with ore reserves of such large tonnage as to give assurance of long life.

Birch followed through on this suggestion and found that several large low-grade copper properties were desperately in need of capital for development. By December, 1915, he had worked out an amazingly successful program. The Guggenheim Exploration Company was planning to disband and agreed to exchange their Utah Copper shares, representing a 25 percent interest, for 607,000 Kennecott shares, and 96.5 percent ownership of Braden Copper Mines in Chile for 770,000 Kennecott shares. An additional 200,000 shares bought a substantial interest in the Alaska Steamship Company from the Alaska Syndicate, which then dissolved. Thus Birch's corporation gained, in addition to the Alaska copper properties, railroad and steamship line, ownership of Braden, the greatest underground copper mine in the world, and

Stephen *Birch* (4th from right) with Kennecott staff. *Courtesy of Alaska and Polar Regions Department, University of Alaska Fairbanks, Helen Von Campon Album acc. 74-27-427*

a quarter interest in Utah Copper, the world's most valuable copper mine, without substantial cash outlay. Following the merger, Edmund A. and Harry F. Guggenheim were listed as additional directors of the Kennecott Copper Corporation.

At the time of its transfer from Guggenheim to Kennecott control, Braden Copper Mines had ore reserves estimated at 220 million tons at 2.2 percent copper and urgently needed cash to build a plant to develop these great reserves. Kennecott supplied the cash over the next several years with earnings from Alaska mines. Utah Copper, in 1915, had ore reserves of 340 million tons at 1.45 percent copper, and also owned 50 percent of Nevada Consolidated Copper shares. In 1916 and 1917, Birch borrowed $16,000,000 in short term notes in order to increase holdings in Utah Copper to 38 percent.

When Kennecott bought the Braden mines, it acquired the services of Earl Tappan Stannard, a brilliant metallurgist who developed an ammonia leaching process to recover additional copper from Bonanza and Jumbo tailings. With Stannard in charge of the mine operation, Birch was able to spend most of his time in New York managing his far-flung financial empire. Although a special cottage at the Kennecott Mines was erected for Birch and his bride in 1916, he rarely visited the Alaska properties after his honeymoon trip.

On June 24, 1916, Birch married Mary Rand, daughter of Rufus R. Rand, president of Minneapolis Gas Light Company. The

Guest house at Kennecott Mine. Built for Birch and his bride in 1916. *Courtesy of Anchorage Museum of History and Art B72-32-16*

wedding party included H.O. Havemeyer II as best man and Percy Rockefeller as an usher. Since the new Mrs. Birch was accustomed to all of the advantages consistent with her family's prominence in Minneapolis, Birch made elaborate preparations for the honeymoon as described in the July 15, 1916 issue of the *Cordova Times*:

> Stephen Birch, accompanied by his bride, arrived at Cordova today on the steamship *Mariposa* on their honeymoon trip, and will remain in the vicinity several weeks.

The private car *Kennecott* has been provisioned and will be at the disposal of Birch and his wife during the time they remain here.

For the accommodation of the bridal couple, the steamship *Mariposa* was remodelled. Several large state-rooms were thrown together, forming an attractive suite, equal in every way to the accommodations usually found in the best hotels on the coast.

The fact that Birch comes north now with his bride in rooms as comfortable as those of an Atlantic liner, and is met at the dock by a private car as finely equipped as any in the world, emphasizes the contrast of conditions as they existed when he first came to Alaska.

Birch mansion, Mahwah, New Jersey. Now the administration building for Ramapo College. *Courtesy of New Jesery State University System*

Apparently these comforts were not sufficient to impress Mary Birch with the glories of Alaska. According to the Cordova paper the following week, the couple reduced their stay to "a flying visit", and there is no record that Mrs. Birch ever returned.

The newlyweds settled in New York City, and soon had two children, Stephen and Mary. According to family sources, the marriage was a difficult one. Stephen, considerably older than his wife, was committed to his business obligations and seldom at home. In 1917 he purchased the 730-acre Theodore Havemeyer estate in Mahwah, New Jersey, near where he had lived as a boy. He introduced game birds for shooting, and utilized the greenhouse for the cultivation of orchids. After his wife Mary died of cancer in 1930, Stephen moved to the Mahwah estate, named Mahrapo Farm, and added a south wing in the form of an old English banquet room with a decorative plaster ceiling and large oak fireplace imported from England. He ran the property as a purebred stock farm, specializing in Guernsey cows and Hampshire sheep, and commuted to his offices in New York City. His sister Emily moved to the farm to care for the two children. Birch became a wealthy man in his own right as a result of several very lucrative years for the copper industry during the first World War. In 1920 he purchased 30,000 acres at Chula Vista, California, near San Diego, which he developed as a haven for horseback riding, bird shooting and stock raising.

The Kennecott Copper Company also prospered, and acquired more property, including the Mother Lode Mine on the other side of the ridge from Bonanza. Jack Smith and Clarence Warner, the original Bonanza locators, staked the Mother Lode in 1906 and attempted to develop it themselves, but did not have adequate capital. When snowslides during the winter of 1919 wiped out their frail tramway, they sold 51 percent of the stock to Birch. A 1,200- foot tunnel, connecting the Mother Lode Mine to the Bonanza workings, extended the life of the Bonanza Mine and enabled Kennecott to process the Mother Lode ore in their own mill, using the Bonanza tramway. Since there was a postwar slump in the price of copper immediately following the war, Birch delayed additional expansion until 1923 when Kennecott paid over a million dollars for the Blackbird mine, which adjoined their Beatson property on LaTouche Island.

Birch's main expansion in 1923, however, was not in Alaska. The Kennecott Copper Company, already owner of 38 percent of the stock in Utah Copper, offered stockholders the option of exchanging one share of Utah stock for one-and-three-quarter shares of Kennecott stock, thus increasing their dividends. At the end of 1923, Birch announced that Kennecott had acquired an additional 628,702 shares of Utah Copper, and owned 76 percent of the stock in that company. Daniel C. Jackling, who developed the process for extracting copper from Utah's large porphyry copper orebody, continued to run the Utah and Nevada mines as a division of the Kennecott Copper Company, and became a director of the corporation.

As the reserves of high-grade ore in Alaska diminished, the Kennecott Copper Company depended more on the larger mines in Utah, Nevada and Chile, and diversified into manufacturing copper and brass products, produced in Chase Brass plants in

Kennecott Mine. 1923 Courtesy of Alaska State Library, PCA210-1

Cleveland and Waterbury, Connecticut. The Alaska mines closed temporarily in 1932 and permanently in 1938. The Copper River and Northwestern Railroad ceased operation when the mines closed, but the Alaska Steamship Company continued to be the main means of transportation to and from Alaska for many years.

Stephen Birch resigned as president of the Kennecott Copper Company in 1933 and was succeeded by E.T. Stannard. Birch continued as Chairman of the Board of Directors and Executive Committee of the company he founded until he died on December 29, 1940, at the age of 68, following abdominal surgery. In addition to his positions with Kennecott, Birch was president and director of the Alaska Steamship Company, chairman of the board of directors of the Braden Copper Company, and a director of the Alaska Development and Mineral Company, the Banker's Trust Company of New York, the Chicago, Burlington and Quincy Railroad Company, the Colorado and Southern Railway Company, and the Northern Pacific Railway Company.

Birch is buried at Ferncliff Mausoleum, Hartsdale, New York, as is his son and his brother, George Howard Birch, former owner of the Dan Creek mines, but not his wife. A stained glass window, depicting Alaskan mountain scenery, adorns their mausoleum.

Who Was Who in America provides the following summary:

> In the year of Birch's death the company employed 28,872 and had sales of $177,250,036. At this time Kennecott also had mining developments in New Mexico, Arizona and South American countries. Under Birch's direction the Kennecott corporation became the largest copper producer in America and the second largest fabricator of copper. Its properties held an estimated 14 percent of the world's copper, and at capacity it was capable of producing 1,000,000,000 pounds of copper annually.

Stained glass window in the Stephen Birch room. *Courtesy of William W. Collins, great nephew of Stephen Birch*

GHOST TOWN — 1938

The Kennecott Copper Company continued to be a major United States copper producer for years following the death of its founder. In Alaska, however, the name Kennecott invokes visions of the state's largest and most spectacular ghost town, with deteriorating barn-red buildings set in breathtaking mountain scenery. The figure of Stephen Birch remains as ghostly as the town he created. During his lifetime Birch shunned publicity. Even in years when the Kennecott Mines were Alaska's major industry *The Alaska Weekly* needed to remind readers who Birch was in the following March 23, 1923 article:

> A metropolitan newspaper the other day made causal mention of the fact that Stephen Birch had given $2,000 toward a fund for the purchase of a library for the Agricultural College and School of Mines at Fairbanks, Alaska.
>
> And the casual reader will probably ask, "Who is Stephen Birch?"
>
> Stephen Birch is the father of copper production in Alaska; he is the man who made one of the world's greatest copper mines out of a great prospect; the man primarily responsible for the building of the Copper River and Northwestern railroad; the man who put the prosperous town of Cordova on the map; the man who made possible the establishment of one of the big steamship lines now plying between this port (Seattle) and Alaskan ports. In short,

he is one of the big constructive figures in the industrial life of Alaska.

Birch rarely gave interviews or had his picture taken. An article in the May 23, 1921 issue of *The Financial World* described him as "husky" and "redheaded." Edward Morgan, a purser for the Alaska Steamship Company, gives the following description of Birch in *God's Loaded Dice*:

Of all the many sourdoughs I have met in my thirty years in the North, Birch was the most romantic and inscrutable figure. Thirty-odd years ago a prospector warming his beans in a skillet over a fire on the Arctic trail, he became a millionaire many times over, a power only less potent in the political world than in the mining world, and the most outstanding personality in all Alaska. Yet in New York, where he worked eighteen hours a day when not traveling over the country inspecting his vast properties, his name meant less to the general public than that of a fairly prosperous broker in Wall Street. And that was as Stephen Birch would have it. Years ago Jack London and Rex Beach told me that, attracted by the glamor of his Alaskan exploits, they had asked Birch's permission to write his life. He refused them with so much finality that they did not insist.

I can well imagine the icy decisiveness of his tones as he refused, for there was something of the Arctic in the chill of his manner. That this was exterior I am convinced through my observations of him over the years, and in this opinion others, who knew him better than I, concur. George Esterly, who prospected with him in the early days, has often told me that Birch was the best fellow in the world as a companion when there were only the two of them, that he always rowed his weight, cheerfully did his share of the cooking, dishwashing, and the rustling and cutting of firewood. It was different, however, whenever a third person joined them. Then he would shut up like a clam, withdraw within himself, and maintain a cold and silent attitude.[37]

Katherine Wilson gives a similar description of Birch in *Copper Tints*:

> Reserved and taciturn, somewhat aloof except with his companions of the trail and his close associates in business, Stephen Birch is personally little known. Today one of the financial powers of New York City, he shuns publicity and evades acclaim as a "captain of industry." Strict to the last penny in the observance of his own obligations, he expects the same of others. But to those that know him best he is a man of deep and broad humanity, inspired in all that he does by a keen sense of his responsibility to the national welfare. With his intimates he is a finely perceptive and generous friend, of an unshakable loyalty.
>
> If the highest type of citizen is that man who, through his vision, his initiative, his constructive power and personal integrity, produces the means by which thousands of others are enabled to live and prosper and the nation is advanced in wealth and power, then Stephen Birch, born Anglo Saxon and self-made man, is an outstanding American.[38]

This reference to Birch as "Anglo Saxon," and other details of his private life, suggests that he may have envisioned himself more as an English country gentleman than as a captain of American industry. Rugged Alaskan sourdoughs may have had difficulty understanding an Anglophile who insisted on strong tea and objected to cigarette smoke,[39] but negative comments usually came from people, like Herman Barring, who lost out to Birch in the lawsuit over the Bonanza claims. Barring referred to him as "an all-around schemer" when testifying before the House Committee on Territories in 1908.

Although the Kennecott Corporation has been criticized for not investing profits in further Alaska development, Birch can scarcely be faulted for reacting to the unfavorable political climate in Alaska after the Pinchot-Ballinger controversy and Wickersham's attacks on the Alaska Syndicate. As Martin Harrais, a frustrated miner himself, wrote in his unpublished manuscript *Gold Lunatics*:

> There comes a point beyond which human nature cannot, or will not, stand abuse, either physical or mental. The unjust character assassination was hell throughout the entire time the Alaska Syndicate was constructing the railroad and Stephen Birch was developing the mine — spending millions of dollars in good faith. The reaction came. The road was not completed as per original plan. They were through with developing Alaska and gave up, no doubt, in disgust. The tradition still lives in the Copper River Valley that it was the avowed policy of the Corporation that they would never spend another dollar in the development of Alaska. This may be only tradition, but it conforms closely to history. They took their profits and bought Utah Copper Co. stock and others; they even took millions of Alaska-made money and invested it in Chile — a South American-revolution-infested country — and considered it safer than investing in Alaska. The irony of it!

Review of sources provides ample evidence that the Alaska Syndicate initially had aspirations that transcended personal profit from the copper mines. Even after the character assassination during the Pinchot-Ballinger controversy, John N. Steele, speaking for the Alaska Syndicate, told the House Committee on Territories:

> The idea in building this road to the Bonanza Mines was to get that country developed. Where we have looked, and where we will look, for the ultimate profit on this road, if there is ever going to be any profit, is the development of Alaska up in the Chitina and Tanana Valleys, where they will be permanently settled, where people will go and raise families and devote themselves to agriculture, because those val-

leys are entirely suited for the raising of a great many crops. That is where we expect to get our permanent returns from the road if we ever get any. The tonnage of the Bonanza Mine is comparatively small, although the ore is very high in copper.[40]

The investment in Utah and South American mines did not occur until after President Woodrow Wilson turned down J.P. Morgan's offer to sell the Copper River and Northwestern Railroad to the federal government for far less than the cost of construction. Delegate Wickersham and the muckraking press had been so successful in slandering the Alaska Syndicate that the President ignored Secretary of Interior Lane's advice to buy the railroad for fear that any negotiation with the notorious Morgans or Guggenheims would cause adverse public reaction.

Melody Webb Grauman, attempting to compare the approach of the Kennecott Copper Corporation to that of the Alaska Syndicate, wrote in her monograph *Big Business in Alaska*:

> The Alaska Syndicate, comparable to the early Rockefeller and Carnegie enterprises, typified the nineteenth century business organization and tactics. Kennecott Copper Corporation, on the other hand, applied the methods and philosophy of twentieth century business management. This interesting contrast becomes fascinating when it is recognized that essentially the same people directed and controlled both organizations — Stephen Birch and the Guggenheims.
>
> The basic goals of both organizations were to keep down production costs and raise copper prices. The Syndicate employed political means to achieve these business goals. As a result, threatened politicians lashed back crying "monopolism." Kennecott adroitly succeeded by controlling labor, acquiring competitive mines, and ensuring a ready market.

Actually the Kennecott Copper Corporation escaped the problems faced by the Alaska Syndicate mainly because Wickersham changed his tactics. By 1915 Wickersham realized that the preservationist policies of Gifford Pinchot were retarding the development of Alaska. Since his political position was secure and his bill to establish an Alaska legislature had passed, the delegate did not need to attack Kennecott Copper Company. Wickersham and Pinchot had created the "Guggenmorgan" monster to serve their own political ambitions. There is little evidence that the Alaska Syndicate tried to control Alaska politics or that it opposed self-government in Alaska. John W. Corson, the candidate that Birch and Jarvis supported in the 1908 delegate election, actually advocated "home rule" for Alaska long before Wickersham decided to espouse that cause.

Although he mercilessly attacked other officials of the Alaska Syndicate, Wickersham usually spoke well of Birch. In his book *Old Yukon, Tales, Trails and Trials* he referred to Birch as a "bright-eyed young man," and a Wickersham letter, written to Ernest Gruening in 1938 in an attempt to forestall closure of the Copper River and Northwestern, contained the following analysis:

> One should not underestimate Mr. Birch's ability as a financier and high grade business man, even on Wall Street. While he organized the Morgan-Guggenheim Alaska Syndicate, he was not a mere employee therein — he was the third member of the Syndicate and furnished the ideas and rules upon which its copper trust and business was based. He furnished these ideas and plans and carried them to success, while the New York partners merely furnished capital.[41]

H. DeWitt Smith summed up Birch's career in a speech at a 1954 regional meeting of the American Institute of Mining Engineers in Salt Lake City:

> Stephen Birch had the ability, unusual in a mining engineer, to sell himself the presidency of Kennecott Mines Company when he made the deal between the Alaska Syndicate and the original prospectors, and the financial acumen to utilize the timely high-grade ore production of this small Alaskan mine to acquire complete control for Kennecott Copper Cor-

poration of the great mines in the United States and Chile which now make Kennecott the largest and most profitable copper company in the world.[42]

Stephen Birch accomplished this in spite of widespread condemnation of his associates and their projects. He shunned publicity, thus escaping character assassination by the muck-raking press, but the attacks must have embittered him and influenced his future interest in Alaska.

In 1910, when Birch wrote an article, entitled "Pioneering Capital," for the *Alaska-Yukon Magazine* he spoke in glowing terms of the development potential in Alaska both in mineral exploration and agriculture. He argued that pioneering capital was still needed to finance lode mining and build railroads in Alaska as it had in the Far West a half century before. Although Birch foresaw greater governmental involvement in the future, he stated that "the progress of Alaska is a flagrant tale of those things which the government has left undone."

At the close of this article, Birch gave his analysis of the dichotomy that would haunt governmental policy in Alaska for the rest of the century:

A public recognition of the fact that there are these two sides in the whole question of conservation and development, each of the utmost importance, will go far toward a more equitable solution than is promised in unthinking antagonism to all large industrial enterprise.[43]

ENDNOTES

(1) - L.A. Levensaler to W.E. Dunkle, June 6, 1953. Polar Collections, U.A.F., Fairbanks.

(2) - Ibid.

(3) - Abercrombie, W.R. *Copper River Exploring Expeditions*, 1899, pg.11.

(4) - Sullivan, Michael Sean. *Kennecott, Alaska - A Historic Preservation Plan*, pg.17

(5) - Wickersham, James. Copper River Mining Co. v. McClellan et al., Nov. 23, 1903 in Alaska Reports, Vol. 2, pgs.137-8.

(6) - Ibid, pg.139.

(7) - Stephen Birch to Governor Ernest Gruening, January 1940 in *Territorial Governor's Papers*. U.S. Government Archives, Seattle .

(8) - Stephen Birch to H.O. Havemeyer Jr., Dec. 2, 1900. Kennecott Library, Salt Lake City, Utah.

(9) - Stephen Birch to D.S. Kain, Jan. 24, 1901. Kennecott Library.

(10)- D.S. Kain to Stephen Birch, Feb. 1, 1901. Kennecott Library.

(11)- Stephen Birch to H.O. Havemeyer Jr., March 9, 1902. Kennecott Library.

(12)- Stephen Birch to H.O. Havemeyer Jr., Nov. 9, 1903. Kennecott Library.

(13)- Nichols, Jeanette Paddock. *Alaska*, pg.269.

(14)- *The Alaska Weekly*, Seattle, March 14, 1924.

(15)- McDonald, Lucille. "John Rosene 's Alaska Activities" in *The Sea Chest*, Vol.10, June 1977, pg.136.

(16)- Stephen Birch to Judge James Wickersham, March 26, 1906. Wickersham Papers, Box 8, Alaska State Historical Library, Juneau.

(17)- *Seattle Post-Intelligencer*, March 8, 1910.

(18)- Shearin, Michael. "William Ross Rust and His Tacoma Legacy." Unpublished manuscript. Washington State Historical Society, Tacoma .

(19)- *The Sea Chest*, Vol.10, June 1977, pg.140.

(20)- Stephen Birch to Judge James Wickersham, April 8, 1907. Wickersham Papers, Box 8. A.S.H.L., Juneau.

(21)- Stephen Birch to Judge James Wickersham, June 3, 1907. Wickersham Papers, Box 8. A.S.H.L., Juneau.

(22)- W.B. Hoggatt to James R. Garfield and Theodore Roosevelt, Sept. 13, 1907. *Territorial Governor's Papers* on microfilm, U.A.A. Archives, Anchorage.

(23)- Stephen Birch to Hon. James Wickersham, Nov. 15, 1907. Wickersham Papers, Box 8. A.S.H.L., Juneau.

(24)- James Wickersham to Stephen Birch, Dec. 19, 1907. Wickersham Papers, Box 14. A.S.H.L., Juneau.

(25)- James Wickersham to Stephen Birch, Feb. 1, 1908. Wickersham Papers, Box 14. A.S.H.L., Juneau.

(26)- Stephen Birch to James Wickersham, March 17, 1908. Wickersham Papers, Box 14. A.S.H.L., Juneau.

(27)- James Wickersham to Stephen Birch, Esq., April 8, 1908. Wickersham Papers, Box 14. A.S.H.L., Juneau.

(28)- Stephen Birch to James Wickersham, Esq., May 6, 1908. Wickersham Papers, Box 14. A.S.H.L., Juneau.

(29)- Stephen Birch to James Wickersham, Esq., May 11, 1908. Wickersham Papers, Box 14. A.S.H.L., Juneau.

(30)- D.H. Jarvis to Honorable James Wickersham, June 24, 1908. Wickersham Papers, Box 14. A.S.H.L., Juneau.

(31)- Stephen Birch to James Wickersham, July 6, 1908. Wickersham Papers, Box 14. A.S.H.L., Juneau.

(32)- Stephen Birch to James Wickersham, Sept. 9, 1908. Wickersham Papers, Box 14. A.S.H.L., Juneau.

(33)- Harrais, Martin. *Gold Lunatics*. Unpublished manuscript. Polar Collections, Rasmusson Library, U.A.F., Fairbanks, pg.212.

(34)- Lewis A. Levensaler. "Early Days of Kennecott, Alaska - as told to Henry C. Carlisle." Polar Collections, U.A.F., Fairbanks, pg.4.

(35)- Smith, H. Dewitt. "Early Days of Kennecott Copper Corporation." Unpublished manuscript. Kennecott Library, Salt Lake City.

(36)- L.A. Levensaler to Ralph McKay, July 10, 1966. Polar Collections, U.A.F., Fairbanks.

(37)- Morgan, Edward E.P. *God's Loaded Dice*, pgs.256-7.

(38)- Wilson, Katherine. *Copper Tints*, pgs.43-4.

(39)- Janson, Lone. *The Copper Spike*, pg.16.

(40)- Statement of John N. Steele before the House Committee on the Territories, Feb. 16, 1911. *Copper River and Northwestern Railway in Alaska*, pg.36.

(41)- James Wickersham to Hon. Ernest Gruening, Nov. 23, 1938. Wickersham Papers, Box 44. A.S.H.L., Juneau.

(42)- Smith, H. Dewitt. "Early Days of Kennecott Copper Corporation." Kennecott Library, Salt Lake City.

(43)- Birch, Stephen. "Pioneering Capital." *Alaska-Yukon Magazine*, Vol.IX, No.5, April 1910, pg.300.

BIBLIOGRAPHY

Abercrombie, W.R. *Copper River Exploring Expedition* - 1899. U.S. Government Printing Office, 1900.

Arends, Dorothea. *The Guggenheims in Alaska: An Essay*. Masters Thesis, Columbia University, 1936.

Atwood, Evangeline. *Frontier Politics: Alaska's James Wickersham*. Portland. Binford and Mort, 1979.

Birch, Stephen. "Pioneering Capital." *Alaska-Yukon Magazine*, Vol. IX, No.5, April 1910.

Breger, Carpel. "Story of Kennecott Copper." *The Financial World*, May 23, 1921, pgs.893-5; May 30, 1921, pgs.933-6; June 6, 1921, pgs.973-5.

Douglass, William C. *A History of the Kennecott Mines, Kennecott, Alaska*. Anchorage. State of Alaska Division of Parks, 1971.

Grauman, Melody Webb. *Big Business in Alaska: The Kennecott Mines 1898-1938*. Fairbanks. Cooperative Park Studies Unit, University of Alaska, 1977.

Hampton, Benjamin B. "Shall Alaska Become a `Morganheim' Barony?" *Hampton's Magazine*, May 1910, pgs. 631-46.

Harrison, E.S. "What Is the Alaska Syndicate Doing?" *Alaska-Yukon Magazine*, Vol.IX, No.6, May 1910.

Hunt, William R. *North of '53, The Wild Days of the Alaska-Yukon Mining Frontier 1870-1914*. New York. MacMillan Publishing Co., 1974.

Janson, Lone. *The Copper Spike*. Anchorage. Alaska Northwest Publishing, 1975.

Lowe, Lieutenent P.G. "Report: From Valdes Inlet to Belle Isle on the Yukon." *Explorations in Alaska - 1898*. U.S. Government Printing Office.

McDonald, Lucile. "John Rosene 's Alaska Activities." *The Sea Chest*, Vol.10, No.4, June 1977.

Morgan, Edward E.P. *God's Loaded Dice*. Caldwell, Idaho. Caxton Printers, 1948.

Nichols, Jeanette Paddock. *Alaska, A History of its Administration, Exploitation and Industrial Development during that First Half Century Under the Rule of the United States*. Cleveland. Arthur H. Clark Co., 1924.

O'Conner, Harvey. *The Guggenheims*. New York. Covier-Friede, 1937.

Pinchot, Gifford. *Breaking New Ground*. New York. Harcourt-Brace, 1917.

Shiels, Archie W. *The Kennecott Story*. Bellingham, April 11, 1967.

Spude, Robert L.S. and Faulkner, Sandra McDermott. *Kennecott, Alaska*. Anchorage. National Park Service, 1987.

Stearns, Robert Aladen. *The Morgan-Guggenheim Syndicate and the Development of Alaska, 1906-1915*. Ann Arbor. University Microfilm International, 1968.

Sullivan, Micheal Sean. *Kennecott Alaska. A Historic Preservation Plan*. Prepared for the Alaska Historical Society.

Wilson, Katherine. *Copper Tints*. Cordova. Daily Times Press, 1923.

ARCHIVAL SOURCES

Alaska State Historical Library, Juneau, Alaska
   Wickersham State Historic Site Collection, Boxes 8, 14, 30, 31, 44.

Kennecott Corporation Library, Salt Lake City, Utah.
   Letters between Stephen Birch and H.O. Havemeyer Jr. and D.S. Kain.
   Corporate Reports of Kennecott Copper Corporation, 1915-1940.
   Smith, H. DeWitt. "Early Days of Kennecott Copper Corporation."

Polar Collections. Rasmusson Library, University of Alaska Fairbanks.
   Harrais, Martin. *Gold Lunatics*. Unpublished manuscript.
   L.A. Levensaler papers. Vertical file.

University of Alaska Anchorage.
   Territorial Governor's Papers on microfilm in U.A.A. Archives.
   Wickersham Diary on microfilm in U.A.A. Archives.
   Newspapers on microfilm:
   The Alaska Prospector, Valdez.   *Cordova Times*.
   Fairbanks Weekly Times.   *Daily Alaska Dispatch*, Juneau.
   The Alaska Weekly, Seattle .

University of Washington Library, Seattle .
   Microfilm of *Seattle Post-Intelligencer*.

Washington State Historical Society Library, Tacoma .
   Shearin, Michael. *William Ross Rust and His Tacoma Legacy*.
   Unpublished manuscript.

INDEX
Bold Bace Indicates Picture

94